PEACE DIPLOMACY

"A FRIEND IN NEED IS A FRIEND INDEED"

AFGHANISTAN

QUESTIONS

- HOW CAN STATES FOSTER RELIGIOUS VALUES IN A COUNTRY?
- WHAT DO RELIGIOUS BOOKS SAY ABOUT PEACE?
- DO DECEASED RELATIVES SPEAK TO PEOPLE – WHAT EXPERIENCES DO PEOPLE HAVE OF THIS?
- HOW CAN GOVERNMENTS FOSTER PEACE YEARS AFTER A CONFLICT HAS ENDED?
- HOW CAN WARLORDS BRING THEIR SIDES TO PEACE?
- HOW CAN POLITICIANS ESTABLISH THEIR INTEGRITY?
- WHAT CAN DIASPORA SUPPORT THEIR COUNTRY?

IDEAS

- A RELIGIOUS TELEVISION STATION SIMILAR TO ETWN IN THE USA FOR MUSLIMS
- POINT OUT TO MUSLIMS ALL THE GOOD MUSLIM WOMEN HAVE DONE IN THE WORLD
- NEWSPAPERS SHOULD PUBLISH SOME ARTICLES IN OTHER LANGUAGES OF THE COUNTRY
- THE UN SHOULD SUPPORT POLICE IN EVERY COUNTRY ON THE PLANET
- A SMALL MONETARY REWARD FOR PARENTS SENDING THEIR CHILDREN TO SCHOOL
- PEOPLE IN POOR COUNTRIES SHOULD BE ENCOURAGED TO ENJOY THEMSELVES
- MUSLIMS ARE PRETTY INTELLIGENT – THIS IS A BUSINESS IDEA – CREATE "BOARD GAMES" FOR CHILDREN HERE

MANTRA

- ONE GOOD PERSON INSPIRES TEN MORE

ALBANIA

IDEAS

- ALBANIANS WHO HAVE MIGRATED TO ITALY SHOULD TELL THE MEDIA HOW MUCH THEY ARE SUFFERING IN THEIR OWN COUNTRY
- REBUILD ANCIENT MONUMENTS IN THE COUNTRY – YOU COULD DEVELOP THESE INTO TOURISTS CENTERS
- A NATO ARMY COLLEGE IN THE COUNTRY
- THERE SHOULD BE A PEER REVIEW ORGANISATION FOR ALL COUNTRIES IN EUROPE WHETHER THEY ARE IN THE EU OR NOT
- I WOULD ENCOURAGE FORMER COMMUNIST COUNTRIES TO HAVE MORE MUSICIANS

ALGERIA

QUESTIONS

- HOW CAN THE WEST WORK WITH AFRICAN MILITARYS FOR PEACE

IDEAS

- ALLOW PUBLIC PROTESTS OUTSIDE OF CITIES
- IF THERE ARE COUP D'ETATS RELIGIOUS LEADERS IN THE COUNTRY COULD JOIN TOGETHER AND FORM AN OPPOSITION TO IT

MANTRA

- ALGERIAS MILITARY MUST TRAIN MILITARIES IN OTHER COUNTRYS IN DOING GOOD WORKS FOR ORDINARY PEOPLE

ANDORA

IDEAS

- DO NOT HAVE TO HAVE YOUR OWN ARMY – OTHER NATIONS CAN AGREE TO PROTECT YOU

ANGOLA

QUSTIONS

- HOW CAN AFRICAN NATIONS GET THE BEST DEALS FROM MUTINATIONALS
- HOW CAN DIASPORA FOSTER PEACE IN THEIR HOME COUNTRYS
- WHAT CAN PEACEMAKERS DO TO SHARE THEIR EXPERIENCES WITH OTHERS

IDEAS

- NGOS CAN GET INVOLVED IN POLITICS AS AN ORGANISATION

ARGENTINA

QUESTIONS

- WHAT MATTERS MOST TO A COUNTRY – HOW CAN A COUNTRY IDENTIFY THIS AND HELP HERE
- WHAT CRITERIA DOES THE IMF APPLY TO HELPING POORER COUNTRIES
- HOW CAN THE POPE HELP FOSTER HUMAN RIGHTS

IDEAS

- THIS COUNTRY COULD SET UP A "SUPER EMBASSY" IN THE FALKLANDS – A GOOD WAY TO MAKE REPARATION TO THE FALKLANDS ISLANDERS – BRINGING BUSINESS TO THEM

ARMENIA

QUESTIONS

- HOW CAN RELIGIONS SPREAD THEIR WORD TO OTHER COUNTRY'S
- WHAT CAN UNIVERSITIES DO TO HELP OTHER NATIONS
- WHAT SKILLS DO CHURCHES HAVE WHEN IT COMES TO PEACEMAKING

IDEAS

- FRIENDS DO THINGS TO EACH OTHER FOR FREE
- THIS COUNTRY NEEDS TO TRADE RESOURCES FOR TERRITORY WITH AZERBAIJAN

- THE FIRST STEP TO NEGOTIATIONS IS TO IDENTIFY WHAT YOUR SIDE NEEDS AND NOT WHAT IT WANTS
- NO "QUID PRO QUO" – E.G. TERRITORY FOR TERRITORY / LANGUAGE TRAINING FOR LANGUAGE TRAINING

AUSTRALIA

QUESTIONS

- IF I SAY THOSE WHO ARE DOING GOOD MUST DO MORE GOOD – WHAT DOES THAT MEAN TO PEOPLE
- HOW CAN GENEROUS NATIONS ENCOURAGE OTHER COUNTRIES TO CONTRIBUTE MORE TO THE THIRD WORLD

IDEAS

- TELL THEM HOW GOOD THEY ARE – TALK ABOUT TELEVISION SERIES SEEN IN THE WEST – ASK THEM TO WRITE FOR TELEVISION SERIES IN THE WEST

MANTRA

- TRAIN MEDIA IN OTHER COUNTRIES

AUSTRIA

IDEAS

- YOU NEED TO ASK MARY TO "BREAK THEIR HEARTS OF STONE AND GIVE THEM HEARTS FOR LOVE ALONE" THEY SHOULD DESIGNATE CAFES / SHOPS / CINEMAS AS BEING "MIXED RACE" FOR AUSTRIANS AND FOREIGN MIGRANTS

MANTRA

- CONFIDENCE IS NOT ENOUGH TO ENTER HEAVEN YOU MUST BE RELIGIOUS TOO

AZERBAIJAN

QUESTIONS

- WHAT KIND OF LINKS CAN BE FOSTERED BETWEEN NATIONS AND ETHNIC RELATIVES IN OTHER COUNTRYS
- WHAT CAN RESOURCE RICH NATIONS DO TO HELP OTHER THIRD WORLD NATIONS
- CAN YOU GIVE EXAMPLES OF WHAT IS INVOLVED IN REFERENDUMS IN OTHER NATIONS
- WHAT SYMBOLIC GESTURES CAN SIDES TAKE TO FOSTER PEACE BETWEEN SIDES
- WHAT CAN POOR COUNTRYS DO TO FOSTER PEACE IN THE WORLD

IDEAS

- AMNESTY INTERNATIONAL COULD MEET REGULARLY WITH THE AZERBAIJANI PRESIDENT
- NGOS MEETING WITH THE PRESIDENT BEFORE AN ELECTION LISTING THEIR DEMANDS

BAHAMAS

QUESTIONS

- WHAT KIND OF VALUES AND CONCEPTS CAN PEOPLE TAKE FROM OTHER COUNTRY'S

IDEAS

- DO THE POPE AND THE QUEEN WANT TO VISIT OTHER COUNTRIES TOGETHER
- SMALL COUNTRIES SHOULD SPECIALISE IN SPORTS TRAINING

BAHRAIN

QUESTIONS

- HOW CAN SMALL NATIONS ATTRACT TOURISTS TO THEIR COUNTRY
- WHAT ARE THE BEST WAYS FOR REACHING OUT TO MUSLIMS
- HOW DO SMALL NATIONS DEVELOP THEIR EDUCATIONAL SECTORS
- HOW CAN RELIGIOUS NATIONS HELP TACKLE POVERTY

IDEAS

- PICTURES OF WOMEN SHOULD BE ALLOWED ON VOTING CARDS AS LONG AS THEY WEAR THE HIJAB. THE MUSLIM BROTHERHOOD SHOULD COMPROMISE ON THIS.
- A LIBRARY COLLECTING ALL BOOKS PUBLISHED EACH YEAR BY MUSLIM AUTHORS ACROSS THE WORLD

BANGLADESH

QUESTIONS

- HOW CAN NATIONS HELP EACH OTHER TACKLE POVERTY
- SOME NATIONS ARE TOO OPPRESSIVE ON WOMEN – HOW CAN THIS BE CHANGED
- WHAT CAN ORGANISATIONS DO TO TACKLE CORRUPTION – WHAT WOULD BE THE FIRST STEPS

IDEAS

- THIS COUNTRY SHOULD CREATE A LOT MORE NGO'S – BE A CENTER FOR NGO'S IN THE REGION – DOES INDIA WANT TO ASSIST IN THIS – AN ACT OF ALTRUISM – FRIENDS DO THINGS FOR EACH OTHER WITHOUT LOOKING FOR A RETURN
- THE LEADER OF A POLITICAL PARTY IN GOVERNMENT – MUST HAVE SOMEONE ELSE IN THEIR PARTY AS PRIME MINISTER

MANTRA

- POOR PEOPLE SHOULD BE ENCOURAGED TO ENJOY THEMSELVES

BELARUS

QUESTIONS

- SAVE THE ENVIRONMENT IN THE COUNTRY [SALT IN A SOAPY SOLUTION] – RUSSIA SHOULD HELP BELARUS SAVE THE COUNTRY FROM RADIOACTIVE SOIL
- POLITICIANS THAT ARE LEADERS MUST KEEP THEIR EGOS IN CHECK – HOW DO THEY DO THIS – PRAISE THE LITTLE SUCCESSES AND NOT THE BIG ONES
- ENCOURAGE CHILDREN TO SEEK ROLE MODELS IN THE WORLD – CHILDREN SHOULD WRITE TO THEM THEY MAY JUST GET A REPLY

IDEAS

- HOW DO YOU EMPOWER POLITICIANS TO DO THEIR JOB
- WHAT DO YOU DO TO HELP COUNTRYS THAT HAVE SUFFERED A LOT
- WHAT DO YOU THINK – BOTSWANA ONLY ALLOWS IN NGOS THAT IMPLEMENT ITS POLICIES

BELGIUM

IDEAS

- WANTS TO KEEP ITS PEOPLE UNITED – HOW CAN YOU HELP HERE – GET EXAMPLES FROM OTHER DIVIDED COUNTRIES | ONE SIDE BEING TAUGHT BOTH LANGUAGES AND THE OTHER SIDE TAUGHT ONLY THEIR OWN LANGUAGE

BELIZE

IDEAS

- SMALL NATIONS SHOULD EMPLOY THE D'HONDT METHOD OF GOVERNANCE
- SMALL NATIONS COULD USE THE SAME CURRENCY AS BIGGER SURROUNDING NATIONS – A BOOST TO THE ECONOMY TO BOTH

BENIN

QUESTIONS

- WHAT CAN RICH AFRICAN COUNTRYS DO TO HELP THEIR POORER NEIGHBOURS
- WHAT INNOVATIONS HAVE MUSLIM CLERICS MADE IN PREACHING ISLAM AROUND THE WORLD
- CHECK OUT THE COMPETITION – WHAT IDEAS WOULD YOU TAKE FROM OTHER RELIGIONS

IDEAS

- COUNTRYS WITH DEEP WATER HARBOURS COULD BECOME MAJOR INTERNATIONAL PORTS
- AU AS AN INSTITUTION SHOULD BAN FEMALE CIRCUMCISION

BHUTAN

IDEAS

- RECORDED VIDEOS OF BUDDHIST MONKS
- CREATIVITY SHOULD BE ENCOURAGED AT ALL AGES – THIS IS THE FUTURE OF HUMANITY SIMPLE TASKS LIKE WEAVING / KNITTING ETC.

BOLIVIA

QUESTIONS

- HOW CAN GOVERNMENTS HELP MINORITIES AND INTEGRATE THEM INTO SOCIETY

IDEAS

- ACKNOWLEDGE GOOD DEEDS DONE BY MINORITIES
- PRESIDENCY – HOW CAN YOU ESTABLISH THE INTEGRITY OF THIS POSITION

BOSNIA

QUESTIONS

- HOW CAN ETHNIC GROUPS INFLUENCE THEIR HOME COUNTRYS
- WHAT CAN POLITICAL PARTIES DO IN OTHER COUNTRYS
- MAYBE BOSNIA IS NOT A MEMBER OF THE EU BUT WHAT CAN IT ADOPT FROM THE EU TO HELP BRING IT CLOSER TO THE EU
- HOW IMPORTANT IS CULTURE TO AN ETHNIC GROUP – CAN YOU GIVE EXAMPLES

IDEAS

- FORCING A COUNTRY TO MAKE REPARATIONS FOR WRONGS COMMITTED DOES NOT HELP BRING PEACE
- THE POPE SHOULD SET UP A SUPER EMBASSY HERE [POPE WOULD BE RESIDENT HERE FOR TWO WEEKS EACH YEAR]
- LOVE IS MORE IMPORTANT THAN BEING RIGHT

MANTRA

- LOVE IS MORE IMPORTANT THAN BEING RIGHT

BOTSWANA

QUESTIONS

- HOW CAN AFRICAN COUNTRIES GET ASSISTANCE FROM WESTERN NATIONS

IDEAS

- NEEDS TO BE ENCOURAGED TO ALLOW NGOS HAVE MORE INDEPEDENCE IN HOW THEY SPEND THEIR MONEY IN THE COUNTRY
- THIS COUNTRY NEEDS ACCESS TO THE COAST – COULD HAVE A ROUTE TO THE COAST AND ESTABLISH AN "ENCLAVE" PORT OWNED BY THEM

BRAZIL

QUESTIONS

- WHAT CAN THE DEVELOPED WORLD DO TO SAVE THE RAINFORESTS
- IF COUNTRYS END THEIR ARMS INDUSTRY – HOW CAN THEY DEAL WITH THE LOSS OF INCOME – WHAT CAN THEY DO WITH THIS INDUSTRY FOR CIVILIAN PURPOSES

IDEAS

- THE UN NEEDS TO SPREAD ITS WINGS AND GET MORE INVOLVED WITHIN INDIVIDUAL COUNTRIES
- UNESCO SHOULD SET UP IN EVERY COUNTRY ON THE PLANET
- BUILDING CAPITALS IN REMOTE AREAS IS NOT A GOOD IDEAS

BULGARIA

QUESTIONS

- HOW CAN POLICE OFFICERS HELP POORER COUNTRYS

IDEAS

- NEEDS TO BE HELPED EXPAND BEYOND TOBACCO TO TEA AND COFFEE PRODUCE
- CHANGE FROM TOBACCO TO HEMP – THIS IS GOING TO BE A HUGE MARKET IN EUROPE – THERE IS A LOT OF RESEARCH GOING INTO HEMP PRODUCTS BY THE EU. THIS COUNTRY HAS THE RIGHT ENVIROMENT TO DO THIS.
- TRAIN PEOPLE AS NETWORK ADMINISTERS – THERE IS GOING TO BE A LARGE SHORT-FALL IN THE NUMBER OF THESE WORKERS OVER THE NEXT 20 YEARS

BURKINA FASO

IDEAS

- DEVELOPED WORLD PHARMACEUTICAL COMPANIES COULD PRODUCE MEDICINES FOR AFRICAN DISEASES FOR FREE. NGO GROUPS COULD LOBBY THEM FOR THIS
- AFRICAN GOVERNMENTS SHOULD ALLOW AMBASSADORS FROM OTHER COUNTRIES SUPERVISE / MEDIATE THE SALE OF MINING RIGHTS – THIS WOULD HELP FIGHT CORRUPTION.
- PROVIDING MEALS AT SCHOOL FOR CHILDREN COULD ENCOURAGE PARENTS TO SEND THEIR COUNTRIES TO SCHOOL. IN CASE OF A FAMINE INTERNATIONAL AID AGENCIES COULD DISPENSE FOOD AT THESE SCHOOLS

BURMA

QUESTIONS

- BURMA NEEDS TO BREAK THE RULES – I KNOW THEY ARE A CONSERVATIVE COUNTRY BUT WHAT CAN THEY CHANGE TO RESPOND TO REQUESTS FROM OTHER DEVEOPED COUNTRYS
- JUDICIARY IS AN IMPORTANT POSITION – HOW CAN YOU PRESERVE ITS INTEGRITY AND WHO DECIDES HOW TO APPOINT THEM

IDEAS

- WHEN IT COMES TO POORER COUNTRYS I WOULD REMIND THE DEVELOPED WORLD WHAT WILLIAM WILBERFORCE ONCE SAID "YOU MAY LOOK THE OTHER WAY BUT YOU CAN NEVER SAY AGAIN THAT YOU DID NOT KNOW"
- LEADERSHIP TRAINING – KEEP AFFIRMING THAT A PERSON IS MAKING THE RIGHT DECISIONS AND EVENTUALLY THEY WILL MAKE THE RIGHT DECISIONS
- A CENTRAL CITY FOR EACH INDIGENOUS GROUP IN THE COUNTRY
- AS A CONFIDENCE BUILDING MEASURE – ALLOW FOREIGN POLITICIANS VISIT POLITICAL PRISONERS IF THIS IS THE START OF PEACE

BURUNDI

QUESTOIONS

- WHAT PRACTICES CAN BE ADOPTED BY FROM TRIBAL / CLANS AND ELDERS TO BRING PEACE
- WHAT PRECEDENTS CAN BE GAINED FROM HISTORY
- WHAT WERE THE INITIAL POSITIONS OF CONFLICTING PARTIES
- WHEN MAKING PEACE – WHAT POWERS CAN BE GIVEN TO POLITICAL LEADERS WHO ARE NOT IN GOVERNMENT

IDEAS

- AN EARLY WARNING NGO IN THE WEST FOR AFRICAN COUNTRYS EXPERIENCING TURMOIL / INSTABILITY
- AFRICAN COUNTRY'S SHOULD VISIT THE WEST AND LIST OUT WHERE THEY NEED HELP
- INTERNATIONAL COUNTRYS COULD HELP ESTABLISH SAFE ZONES WITHIN HOME COUNTRYS FOR REFUGEES
- ALL POLITICAL LEADERS CAN GO ANYWHERE IN THE COUNTRY – THEY ARE GIVEN PROTECTION
- I RECKON THIS COUNTRY IS RELIGIOUS – IT SHOULD HAVE SOME RELIGIOUS LEADERS AS ADVISORS TO THE PRESIDENT

CAMBODIA

QUESTIONS

- HOW DO YOU DEAL WITH LEADERS WHO ARE CORRUPT
- WOULD FRENCH SPEAKING NATIONS BENEFIT FROM EACH OTHER AND HOW
- HOW CAN CHINA HELP OTHER NATIONS DEAL RESPONSIBLY WITH THEIR NATURAL RESOURCES

IDEAS

- FOR PEACE WITH THE KHMER ROUGE THERE SHOULD BE MILITARY TO MILITARY PEACE TALKS
- A BUSINESS COMMUNITY THAT CAN LOBBY POLITICIANS AND SPEAK IN PARLIAMENT

CAMEROON

IDEAS

- THE PRESIDENT SHOULD BE INVOLVED IN CULTURAL ACTIVITIES IN HIS COUNTRY
- GET ALL CHRISTIAN CHURCHES TO ACCEPT THE CONCEPTQUESTIONS

CANADA

QUESTIONS

- HOW CAN CANADA HELP OTHER COUNTRYS WITH MINORITIES AND REFUGEES

CENTRAL AFRICAN REPUBLIC

QUESTIONS

- HOW CAN REFUGEES HELP THEIR OWN COUNWITHWHEN AND HOW SHOULD REBEL LEADERS WHO ARE A THREAT TO THE GOVERNMENT BE DEALT WITH

- WHAT STANDARD MEASURES COULD THE AQUEMUYING WITH COUP D'ETAT'S

- WHAT METHODS ARE BEING USED IN OTHER COUNTRYS TO DEAL WITH THEM

IDEAS

- IT HAS TO BE A PRIORITY FOR THE DEVELOPED WORLD TO TACKLE THE SPREAD OF DESERTS IN THE WORLD

- A NEWSLETTER PRODUCED IN AFRICA AND DISTRIBUTED TO GOVERNMENTS IN THE DEVELOPED WORLD
- THE PRESIDENT SHOULD MEET HIS VICTIMS – IF SOMEONE REALLY GOOD TALKED TO HIM HE MIGHT CHANGE – HIS WIFE NEEDS TO MAKE DEMANDS OF HIM. SHE COULD RECEIVE PEOPLE WHO HAVE BEEN VICTIMS OF HIS POLICIES. WIFE TOGETHER WITH HUSBAND SHOULD ASK HOW THEY CAN MAKE AMENDS.
- MIXED RELIGION MARRIAGES – FIRST CHILD IS ONE RELIGION AND THE NEXT IS FROM THE OTHER RELIGION – THIS IS BEING DONE IN ETHIOPIA – WHERE MOHAMMAD FLED WITH HIS FOLLOWERS FROM PERSECUTION

CHAD

QUESTIONS

- WHAT POLICIES CAN GOVERNMENTS ADOPT TO EMPOWER PEOPLE
- WHAT CAN YOUNG PEOPLE DO TO HELP AFRICA - CAN YOU GIVE EXAMPLES FROM AFRICA

IDEAS

- FOR NEGOTIATING PEACE – A PRESIDENT CAN ACCEPT FORMER REBEL LEADERS AS PRESIDENTIAL ADVISORS ON HIS TEAM
- AFRICAN COUNTRIES SHOULD SEEK TO ABOEXAMPLES .IES LIKE COSTA RICA. FOR SECURITY PURPOSES FOREIGN COUNTRIES COULD ESTABLISH MILITARY BASES HERE – A REAL MONEY EARNER – TO SATISFY MUSLIM CONCERNS THESE BASES SHOULD BE ESTABLISHED OUTSIDE OF TOWNS AND CITIES. RUSSIA COULD DO THIS
- MILITARY BASES SHOULD ALLOW THEIR MEDICAL FACILITIES TO BE OPEN TO THE SURROUNDING COMMUNITIES
- SATELITE PHONES / RADIO TRANSMITTER / MOBILE PHONES AVAILABLE TO ELDERS IN EVERY COMMUNITY IN THE COUNTRY

CHILE

QUESTIONS

- WHAT WOULD MAKE A PERSONS RELIGION MAKE THEM FEEL MOST APPRECIATED
- BUSINESS MATTERS MOST FOR SOME RELIGIONS - HOW CAN THIS BE AN ENTRY POINT FOR PEACE

IDEAS

- A LEADER SHOULD ADOPT THE RELIGION OF A PERSECUTED GROUP TO PROTECT THEM – I DON'T THINK GOD WOULD CONDEMN THIS
- RE: TOURISM – CREATE A FREE CD ABOUT YOUR COUNTRYS ATTRACTIONS AND DISTRIBUTE THEM IN LOCAL LANGUAGES TO TRAVEL AGENCIES AROUND THE WORLD

CHINA

QUESTIONS

- HOW CAN CHINA HELP ECONOMIES OF THIRD WORLD NATIONS
- HOW CAN CHINA MODERATE ITS MEDIA

- JOURNALISTS COULD BE ALLOWED TO USE REUTERS BBC ETC AS SOURCES OF INFORMATION
- HOW CAN CHINAS MILITARY HELP OTHER NATION

IDEAS

- TERRITORIAL DISPUTES - RESOLVED – TERRITORY OR RESOURCES – CONTIGUITY – DIVIDED ALONG NATURAL FEATURES – WHO HAS BEEN THE LONGEST THERE OVER THE LAST 100 YEARS – REWARDS FOR ACHIEVING PEACE BY THE INTERNATIONAL COMMUNITY
- SIMPLE AND SHORT LETTERS BY CAMPAIGNERS TO POLITICIANS WORK BEST
- DOES CHINA WANT TO INTRODUCE CREDIT UNIONS – MY REWARD FOR HELPING THEM IS THAT THEY HELP SET UP CREDIT UNIONS ALL OVER THE THIRD WORLD

MANTRA

- THIS COUNTRY CAN HAVE MORE CHILDREN

COLOMBIA

QUESTIONS

- IF THE CHURCH WAS TO APPLY THE MANTRA - "BREAK THE RULES" FOR PEACE WHAT WOULD THIS ENTAIL

IDEAS

- POLICE ROLE MODELS
- THE CATHOLIC CHURCH SHOULD BE RESPONSIBLE FOR MONITORING HUMAN RIGHTS – THEY SHOULD LIST THE NAMES OF DISSAPEARED / MURDERED PEOPLE AT MASS – OSCAR ROMERO DID SOMETHING SIMILAR IN EL SALVADOR
- HEMP PRODUCTS GOOD FOR THE ENVIRONMENT – THE EU WOULD BE A MAJOR MARKET FOR THIS – THIS COULD REPLACE THE DRUGS TRADE – EVERYTHING FROM OIL TO PAPER TO COSMETICS

REPUBLIC OF CONGO

QUESTIONS

- POVERTY IS A BIG ISSUE IN THIRD WORLD COUNTRIES - WHAT EXAMPLES ARE THERE IN OTHER THIRD WORLD COUNTRIES FOR DEALING WITH THIS
- HOW CAN RELIGION BE USED TO PROMOTE PEACE

IDEAS

- A LANGUAGES COLLEGE TO ATTRACT PEOPLE FROM ALL OVER AFRICA
- DON'T TRY TO PLEASE EVERYONE IF YOU DO YOU END UP PLEASING NO ONE
- COULD SOMEONE WHO QUESWORLDLEADER FOR TOO LONG TAKE UP A NEW ROLE AS KING – WITH A ROYAL FAMILY. THIS WOULD BE A CEREMONIAL ROLE. IT MAY FREE UP MANY UN-DEMOCRATIC COUNTRIES. FOR REFERENCE THE EXAMPLE CHOSEN WOULD BE THE ROLE OF THE ROYAL FAMILY IN THE UK. THE GOVERNMENT DECIDES THE BUDGET FOR THIS KING.

COSTA RICA

QUESTIONS

- HOW CAN THE COMMONWEALTH CONTRIBUTE TO PEACE IN THE WORLD
- WHAT HAS THE QUEEN DONE TO CONTRIBUTE TO PEACE IN THE WORLD

IDEAS

- SETTING UP MORE PEACE COLLEGES IN THE COUNTRY
- THIS COUNTRY HAS NO ARMY – AND IT SHOULD ENCOURAGE OTHER COUNTRIES AROUND THE WORLD TO DO LIKEWISE
- BREAK THE RULES – THIS COUNTRY SHOULD BE ALLOWED TO JOIN THE COMMONWEALTH – THE QUEEN COULD VISIT THIS COUNTRY

COTE D'IVOIRE

IDEAS

- PRISONERS CAN VOTE IN ELECTIONS – INCLUDING REBEL MEMBERS
- YOU WOULD BE BETTER OFF OWING DEBT TO YOUR OWN COUNTRY SUCH AS TO BANKS WITHIN YOUR COUNTRY
- DO RESEARCH INTO USING STRAW TO CLEAN RIVERS AND GET RID OF POLLUTION

CROATIA

IDEAS

- ASK GOD TO "BREAK THEIR HEARTS OF STONE AND GIVE THEM HEARTS FOR LOVE ALONE" PRAY FOR THIS
- RE-INSTATE THE ROYAL FAMILY IN THIS COUNTRY – THE QUEEN FROM THE UK COULD HELP HERE – BREAK THE RULES HERE – I THINK PEOPLE IN THE WORLD WITH ROYALTY LOVE THEM MORE THAN POLITICIANS SUCH AS PRESIDENTS
- FOREIGN COUNTRIES NGOS SHOULD TARGET THIS COUNTRY AROUND ELECTION TIME TO WORK FOR A MODERATE PARLIAMENT
- NGOS SHOULD MEET WITH THE PRESIDENT AROUND ELECTION TIME WITH A LIST OF DEMANDS
- CREATE FREE ENCLAVES WHERE FOREIGN INDUSTRIES CAN SET UP – NO TAXES AT ALL

CUBA

QUESTIONS

- HOW CAN RELIGIOUS LEADERS INFLUENCE CHANGE IN COMMUNIST COUNTRIES
- HOW CAN WESTERN GOVERNMENTS MAKE AMENDS FOR THEIR PAST TREATMENT OF CUBA
- HOW CAN THE POWER OF LOVE BE USED TO CHANGE LEADERS OPINIONS

IDEAS

- CUBA COULD SPECIALISE IN PROVIDING MEDICAL ASSISTANCE TO OTHER CENTRAL AMERICAN NATIONS – I THINK THEY WOULD BE PRETTY HAPPY TO DO THIS – IN RETURN THE US COULD AGREE TO CEASE CLAIMING CUBAN BUSINESSES
- CUBA COULD OPEN ITS HEALTHCARE SYSTEM TO TOURISTS FROM ABROAD

CYPRUS

QUESTIONS

- HOW CAN THE EU AFFECT FOREIGN POLICY IN ITS NEIGHBOURING STATES

IDEAS

- IF A PERSON IS REALLY GOOD THEY CAN INFLUENCE OTHERS

CZECH REPUBLIC

IDEAS

- ENCOURAGE THEM TO LEARN THE LANGUAGES OF THEIR NEIGHBOURING COUNTRIES
- THIS COUNTRY SHOULD MAKE ITS POLICY TO MAKE FRIENDS WITH OTHER CONSERVATIVE COUNTRIES IN THE WORLD AND SPECIFICALLY ONLY THEM
- IF THIS COUNTRY WANTS TO INCREASE TOURISM NUMBERS IT SHOULD ADVERTISE AND PROMOTE FAMOUS PEOPLE FROM ITS COUNTRY

DEMOCRATIC REPUBLIC OF CONGO

QUESTIONS

- WHAT INCENTIVES CAN BE GIVEN TO REBEL LEADERS TO GIVE UP VIOLENCE
- TRIBAL GROUPS HAVE NO MECHANISMS FOR MIXING WITH EACH OTHER - WHAT CAN BE DONE TO CHANGE THIS
- HOW CAN MULTINATIONAL COMPANIES BE HELD ACCOUNTABLE FOR THEIR ACTIONS IN THIRD WORLD COUNTRIES

IDEAS

- WAGES FOR CIVIL SERVICE / MILITARY / POLICE SHOULD BE PROVIDED BY THE DEVELOPED WORLD
- TRIBES SHOULD BE ALLOWED TO CROSS BOUNDARIES IN EXCHANGE FOR GIVING UP THEIR WEAPONS THE PRESIDENT COULD EMPLOY FORMER REBELS AS PRESIDENTIAL ADVISORS
- ALL POLITICAL LEADERS CAN BE PRESENT AT GOVERNMENT MEETINGS – PROVIDE SUGGESTIONS BUT NOT VOTING

MANTRA

- A FRIEND IN NEED IS A FRIEND INDEED

DENMARK

IDEAS

- HALF OF ALL FAMILIES ARE SINGLE PARENT FAMILIES – PARENTS FROM A GENERATION AGO SHOULD LIVE WITH THEIR CHILDREN [NOW PARENTS] THIS MAY LEAD TO LESS SINGLE PARENTING
- A CENTRAL PRINTING PRESS FOR MORE THAN ONE AGENCY – THIS WOULD ALLOW CHEAPER PUBLICATIONS

MANTRA

- MARRY YOUR BEST FRIEND

DOMINICAN REPUBLIC

QUESTIONS

- HOW CAN NGOS INFLUENCE POLITICAL POWER
- RICH PEOPLE SHOULD BE ENCOURAGED TO BE RICH IN GOOD WORKS - CAN YOU GIVE EXAMPLES OF SUCH PEOPLE
- HOW CAN GOVERNMENTS CHANEL REMITANCES INTO GOOD WORKS

IDEAS

- A LEADER SHOULD REALISE THEY CANNOT SOLVE EVERYTHING – THEIR MANTRA SHOULD BE TO BASES / PRIORITIES / WORTH A SHOT
- THE CHURCH SHOULD SEEK TO TEACH AND RECRUIT POOR PEOPLE INTO THE PRIESTHOOD – MANY YOUNG PEOPLE IN AFRICA SAY THEY WANT TO BE SOMEONE GOOD LIKE A PRIEST

DJIBOUTI

IDEAS

- PRESIDENTIAL ADVISORS – SOMETIMES THERE ARE TOO MANY FACTIONS TO GIVE POWERS TO – ADDITIONAL POSTS COULD BE GIVEN AS PRESIDENTIAL ADVISORS. IN THE US PRESIDENTIAL ADVISORS WORK WITH THE PRESIDENT AND DO NOT SEEK ANY CREDIT FOR THEIR IDEAS.

DOMINICAN REPUBLIC

QUESTIONS

- WHAT CAN GOVERNMENTS DO TO ENCOURAGE RICH PEOPLE TO SHARE THEIR WEALTH WITH GOOD CAUSES
- HOW CAN RELIGIOUS LEADERS REFORM POLITICS
- WHAT CAN BE DONE TO PREVENT MONOPOLIES OF POWER IN POLITICS
- WHAT LOW COST INCENTIVES CAN BE USED TO MAKE A CITY MORE TOURIST FRIENDLY

IDEAS

- THE CARIBBEAN SHOULD SPECIALISE IN PEACE – TRAINING COURSES ON PEACE – NO ARMIES – PEACE COLLEGES
- A CULTURAL EVENT – HOLDING PARADES IN OTHER COUNTRIES WHERE YOU HAVE A LARGE DIASPORA EG ST PATRICK'S DAY PARADES IN THE US
- A "PRISON FELLOWSHIP" FOR LATIN AMERICAN COUNTRIES

EQUADOR

QUESTIONS

- APOLOGIZE FOR POLITICAL ASSASSINATIONS IN THE PAST. THE GOVERNMENT MUST MAKE REPARATIONS FOR THIS TO THE COMMUNITIES WHERE THEY CAME FROM AND NOT TO INDIVIDUALS OR FAMILY MEMBERS
- THE CHURCH COULD SUPPORT ELECTIONS ACROSS A COUNTRY FOR FREE. SOME AFRICAN AND LATIN AMERICAN HAVE HUGE COSTS WHEN IT COMES FOR ELECTIONS

EGYPT

QUESTIONS

- HOW HAVE FORMER TERRORISTS BROUGHT PEACE TO THE WORLD - GIVE EXAMPLES
- HOW HAVE RELIGIOUS LEADERS FOSTERED PEACE BETWEEN MIXED COMMUNITIES
- WHAT KIND OF ACTIVITIES COULD RELIGIOUS LEADERS WORK ON TOGETHER
- WHO ARE THE FIRST MOVERS ON PEACE BETWEEN COMMUNITIES -'GIVE EXAMPLES. GIVE EXAMPLES

IDEAS

- THE FOUR BASES FOR DEVELOPMENT IN AFRICA ARE POLICE, NGOS, WOMEN AND CREDIT UNIONS. FORMER PRIME MINISTER JACK LYNCH STATED THAT NGOS WOULD SAVE THE WORLD
- MUSLIMS LOVE BUILDING MOSQUES – IF THE WEST WANTS TO BUILD PEACE WITH ISLAM THEY SHOULD BUILD MOSQUES FOR THEM

MANTRA

- CREATE RESPECT FOR OTHER RELIGIONS

WHAT DO YOU THINK OF THE FOLLOWING PASSAGE FROM THE BIBLE –

WHEN ALLAH COMES TO JUDGE THE EARTH IN HEAVEN – HE WILL SIT ON HIS GLORIOUS THRONE. BEFORE HIM WILL BE GATHERED ALL THE NATIONS, AND HE WILL SEPARATE PEOPLE ONE FROM ANOTHER AS A SHEPHERD SEPARATES THE SHEEP FROM THE GOATS. AND HE WILL PLACE THE SHEEP ON HIS RIGHT, BUT THE GOATS ON THE LEFT. THEN THE ALLAH WILL SAY TO THOSE ON HIS RIGHT, "COME YOU WHO ARE BLESSED BY MY FATHER, INHERIT THE KINGDOM PREPARED FOR YOU FROM THE FOUNDATION OF THE WORLD. FOR I WAS HUNGRY AND YOU GAVE ME FOOD, I WAS THIRSTY AND YOU GAVE ME A DRINK, I WAS A STRANGER AND YOU WELCOMED ME, I WAS NAKED AND YOU CLOTHED ME, I WAS SICK AND YOU CAME AND VISITED ME, I WAS IN PRISON AND YOU CAME TO ME." THEN THE RIGHTEOUS WILL ANSWER HIM, SAYING "LORD WHEN DID WE SEE YOU HUNGRY AND FEED YOU, OR THIRSTY AND GIVE YOU DRINK" AND WHEN DID WE SEE YOU SICK OR IN PRISON AND VISIT YOU? AND WHEN DID WE SEE YOU A STRANGER AND WELCOME YOU, OR NAKED AND CLOTHE YOU AND WHEN DID WE SEE YOU SICK OR IN PRISON AND VISIT YOU? AND ALLAH WILL ANSWER THEM, "TRULY, I SAY TO YOU, AS YOU DID IT TO ONE OF THE LEAST OF THESE MY BROTHERS, YOU DID IT TO ME."

"THEN ALLAH WILL SAY TO THOSE ON HIS LEFT, "DEPART FROM ME, YOU CURSED, INTO THE ETERNAL FIRE PREPARED FOR THE DEVIL AND HIS ANGELS. FOR I WAS HUNGRY AND YOU GAVE ME NO FOOD, I WAS THIRSTY AND YOU GAVE ME NO DRINK, I WAS A STRANGER AND YOU DID NOT WELCOME ME, NAKED AND YOU DID NOT CLOTHE ME, SICK AND IN PRISON AND YOU DID NOT VISIT ME' THEN THEY ALSO WILL ANSWER, SAYING, "LORD, WHEN DID WE SEE YOU HUNGRY OR THIRSTY OR A STRANGER OR NAKED OR SICK OR IN PRISON, AND DID NOT MINISTER TO YOU?" THEN HE WILL ANSWER THEM, SAYING, "TRULY, I SAY TO YOU, AS YOU DID NOT DO IT TO ONE OF THE LEAST OF THESE, YOU DID NOT DO IT TO ME." AND THESE WILL GO AWAY INTO ETERNAL PUNISHMENT, BUT THE RIGHTEOUS INTO ETERNAL LIFE *

EL SALVADOR

QUESTIONS

- THEIR IS A LOT OF CORRUPTION WITHIN COUNTRIES FROM MAYORS AND PROVINCIAL LEADERS - HOW CAN THIS BE DEALT WITH
- HOW CAN THE MILITARY IMPROVE THE QUALITY OF LIFE WITHIN A COUNTRY ESPECIALLY FOR THE POOR
- WHAT CAUSES COMMUNISTS REBELS – MAJOR SOCIAL JUSTICE ISSUES – GET BACK TO THEIR INITIAL DEMANDS – RECORD THESE AS PRECEDENTS.

IDEAS

- IF THERE IS A CEASEFIRE THEN TWICE A WEEK THESE GUERILLA REBELS SHOULD BE ALLOWED TO GO TO SCHOOL FOR EDUCATION
- POOR COUNTRIES CANNOT AFFORD TO PROVIDE SOCIAL WELFARE ON A PERMANENT BASIS. POOR PEOPLE ARE TRAPPED INTO POVERTY. WHAT COULD BE DONE IS THAT A GOVERNMENT THREE TO FOUR TIMES A YEAR POOR PEOPLE WOULD RECEIVE A BIGGER LUMP SUM.
- RANDOM INVESTIGATIONS INTO CORRUPTION BY BUSINESSES / POLITICIANS / INDIVIDUALS

ERITREA

QUESTIONS

- HOW HAVE FORMER RESTRICTIVE COUNTRIES OPENED UP AND HOW CAN THEY HELP OTHERS TOO
- ALLOW HUMAN RIGHTS GROUPS INTO THIS COUNTRY

IDEAS

- A GOOD WAY FOR COUNTRIES TO OWN A PEACE PROCESS IS FOR MEDIATORS TO PROVIDE OPTIONS FOR THEM TO CHOOSE FROM
- A PRESIDENT CAN GIVE UP HIS ROLE AS LEADER OF THE COUNTRY AND CHOOSE TO BECOME HEAD OF THE MILITARY
- A FIRST STEP IS TO ALLOW POLITICAL PARTIES AT A REGIONAL LEVEL
- ONE MEMBER FROM EACH PRESS AGENCY CAN ENTER A COUNTRY

ESTONIA

QUESTIONS

- HOW CAN RELIGIONS BE USED TO PROMOTE PEACE

IDEAS

- AN ATTORNEY GENERAL WITH POWERS TO SACK POLITICIANS BUT NOT A MEMBER OF A POLITICAL PARTY

ETHIOPIA

QUESTIONS

- HOW CAN GOVERNMENTS BE ENCOURAGED TO FORCE MULTINATIONALS TO MAKE AMENDS TO THIRD WORLD COUNTRIES. WHAT KIND OF PRECEDENTS ARE THERE

- HOW CAN NGOS INFLUENCE CHANGE IN OTHER FOREIGN COUNTRIES. WHAT EXAMPLES CAN YOU GIVE FOR THIS
- WHAT ARE THE VARIOUS WAYS NGOS CAN ATTRACT FUNDING FROM FOREIGN GOVERNMENTS
- HOW CAN NGOS WORK TOGETHER TO INFLUENCE CHANGE IN A COUNTRY

IDEAS

- WHEN IT COMES TO PEACE THE MANTRA IS "COVER ALL BASES"
- IN DEALING WITH BOUNDARIES – DECIDING FACTORS SHOULD BE RESOURCES / TERRITORY OR FOLLOWING TERRAIN SUCH AS ROADS / RIVERS / MOUNTAINS. GO BACK TO BOUNDARIES THAT EXISTED BEFORE ANY CONFLICTS BEGAN.
- FOR THE SAKE OF PEACE A LEADER SHOULD TAKE THE RELIGION OF THE OTHER SIDE
- THERE SHOULD BE HOMELANDS FOR SMALL INDIGENOUS TRIBES
- A TRADING ENCLAVE PURCHASED BY A FOREIGN COUNTRY – THIS COULD BE OF BENEFIT TO BOTH NATIONS
- SAUDI ARABIA SHOULD MAKE A FINANCIAL CONTRIBUTION TO ETHIOPIA EACH YEAR AS A THANK YOU FOR ALLOWING THE PROPHET MOHAMMAD AND HIS FOLLOWERS TO TAKE REFUGE IN THEIR COUNTRY DURING HIS TIME OF DANGER
- IT IS TIME FOR MUSLIM COUNTRIES TO THANK PEOPLE FROM OTHER NATIONS / RELIGIONS WHO HAVE HELPED THEM THROUGHOUT HISTORY
- BREAKAWAY REGIONS CAN HAVE THEIR OWN ARMED POLICE BUT NO ARMY TO STAY WITH A COUNTRY - THE BIGGEST ISSUE FOR SMALL ETHNIC REGIONS IS SECURITY

FIJI

QUESTIONS

- HOW CAN MINORITIES MAKE A DIFFERENCE IN A COUNTRY
- WHAT KIND OF PROBLEMS HAVE MILITARIES CAUSED IN SMALL COUNTRIES
- WHAT CAN BE DONE TO MAKE CITIES MORE TOURIST FRIENDLY
- HOW CAN COUNTRIES MARKET THEMSELVES ABROAD
- I DONT SUPPORT COUP D'ETAT'S - WHAT CAN BE DONE TO REINSTATE DEPOSED LEADERS

IDEAS

- THE JUDICIARY SHOULD CONTROL THE ARMY – THIS MAY HELP PREVENT COUPS
- HAVE WESTERN SHOPS LIKE STARBUCKS AND MCDONALD'S IN YOUR COUNTRY – THIS WOULD BE A MECCA FOR TOURISTS

FINLAND

IDEAS

- ENCOURAGE MORE POLITICAL LEADERS IN FINLAND TO WORK FOR PEACE. SMALL WEALTHY NATIONS CAN GET INVOLVED IN PEACE MEDIATION
- THIS COUNTRY SHOULD CREATE NEW NOBEL PRIZE CATEGORIES – A YOUTH PRIZE / AN AFRICAN POLITICIANS PRIZE / AN NGO PRIZE

FRANCE

QUESTIONS

- HOW CAN FRANCE EMPOWER THIRD WORLD NGOS ESPECIALLY ON PEACE AND HUMAN RIGHTS
- HOW CAN THE EU ASSIST MEDIA IN THIRD WORLD COUNTRIES

IDEAS

- POINT OUT TO FRANCE THAT IT IS NOT AN EGALITARIAN IF IT PREVENTS EXPRESSIONS OF RELIGION. THERE SHOULD BE RELIGIOUS EDUCATION IN SCHOOLS – THIS EDUCATION SHOULD POINT OUT THE GOOD THINGS THAT THE CHRISTIAN / MUSLIM / JEWISH RELIGIONS ARE DOING IN THE WORLD
- FOR YOUR FRIENDS - YOU COULD BUILD STATUES SUCH AS THE STATUE OF LIBERTY IN THEM **MANTRA**
- MUST PROMOTE RELIGIOUS VALUES

GABONESE REPUBLIC

QUESTIONS

- HOW CAN MEDIA ASSIST IN CHANGE IN FOREIGN COUNTRIES

IDEAS

- FOR AFRICAN NATIONS JUST COMING OUT OF CONFLICT – THE UN COULD APPOINT THE HEAD OF THE MILITARY FOR THE GOVERNMENT / AND THE VICE PRESIDENT

GAMBIA

QUESTIONS

- HOW CAN POLICE FORCES ASSIST POOR COUNTRIES
- SOME LEADERS WANT TO STAY IN POWER PERMANENTLY - WHAT INCENTIVES CAN THE INTERNATIONAL COMMUNITY USE TO CHANGE TTHI

IDEAS

- COUNTRIES ACKNOWLEDGE GOOD DEEDS DONE TO THEM BY FOREIGNERS
- JOURNALISTS CANNOT BE JAILED THEY CAN ONLY BE FINED

GEORGIA

QUESTIONS

- HOW CAN POLITICIANS ENSURE THAT THEIR LEADERS MEET CERTAIN STANDARDS
- WHAT CAN BE DONE TO ENCOURAGE YOUNG CHILDREN TO CHOOSE ROLE MODELS IN LIFE

IDEAS

- A SINGLE MILITARY FOR ALL OF GEORGIA – WHAT WILL GEORGIA TRADE OSSETIA AND ABKHAZIA FOR THIS
- DECLARE PEOPLE WHO ARE REALLY GOOD FROM OTHER RELIGION AS SAINTS. MOHAMMAD SHOULD BE DECLARED A SAINT – THIS COULD HELP BRING WORLD PEACE
- PARTNERSHIP FOR PEACE PROGRAMMES BETWEEN THE EU AND THIRD WORLD COUNTRIES THAT REDUCE MILITARY SPENDING

GERMANY

QUESTIONS

- HOW CAN THIS COUNTRY IMPROVE THE WELL-BEING OF SECOND-WORLD COUNTRIES
- CAN YOU GIVE EXAMPLES OF WOMEN WHO HAVE DONE GREAT THINGS IN LIFE

IDEAS

- A PRECEDENTS ORGANISATION – RECORD THE STATEMENTS OF POLITICIANS AND ATTACKERS OVER TIME – TO QUOTE IN PEACE TALKS – POSITIONS THEY TOOK IN THE PAST
- POLITICIANS VISITING THIRD WORLD COUNTRIES AND SPEAKING IN THEIR UNIVERSITIES

MANTRA

- THOSE WHO ARE DOING GOOD MUST DO MORE GOOD IF WE ARE TO SAVE THE WORLD

GHANA

QUESTIONS

- HOW CAN THE AU PROTECT AFRICAN LEADERS

IDEAS

- TOURISTS CAN USE THEIR OWN CURRENCY IN YOUR COUNTRY ON A 1-1 BASIS EVEN IF THERE IS A DIFFERENCE IN EXCHANGE RATES
- LEADER OF A COUNTRY SHOULD HAVE A GET OUT FAST PLAN INCASE OF A COUP D'ETAT. IF THE LEADER ESCAPES THEY WOULD BE ABLE TO WORK WIYH OTHER GOVERNMENTS TO RESTORE PEACE
- AU PEACE-SOLDIERS SHOULD BE THE ONLY SOLDIERS IN THE CAPITAL OF ANY AFRICAN COUNTRY

GREECE

QUESTIONS

- HOW CAN INTERNATIONAL AGENCIES ASSIST GREECE
- HOW CAN GREECE PARTICIPATE IN WORLD POLITICS
- HOW CAN GREECE MAXIMIZE ITS POLITICAL PRESENCE IN OTHER COUNTRIES

IDEAS

- REINSTATING THE ROYAL FAMILY COULD BE A TOURISM ASSET FOR GREECE
- THIS COUNTRY NEEDS TO EXPAND ITS PORTFOLIO OF BRAND NAMES

GUATEMALA

QUESTIONS

- THE LEADER OF A COUNTRY MUST TALK DIRECTLY WITH REBEL PEOPLES – THIS MIGHT WORK FOR DRC / SUDAN AND MYANMAR
- WHAT IS THE BEST WAY TO PROTECT WORLD LEADERS IN A COUP D'ETAT

IDEAS

- IF A LEEADER WANTS TO BE POPULAR AND GET ELECTED HE MUST MEET WITH EVERY GROUP THAT IS NOT MAINSTREAM THIS WOULD MAKE EVERYONE LIKE HIM.

- YOU LOOSE ALL YOUR PROPERTY IF YOU SUPPORT DEATH SQUADS – YOU HAVE TO MAKE IT SO EXPENSIVE FOR RICH LAND OWNERS TO SUPPORT THEM

GUINEA

QUESTIONS

- WHAT QUALITIES SHOULD A POLITICAL LEADER HAVE - WHAT ADVICE WOULD THEY PASS ON TO OTHERS
- HOW CAN THE AU ASSIST OTHER COUNTRIES TO ENSURE THAT MULTINATIONALS TREAT THEM FAIRLY

IDEAS

- NGOS SHOULD BE ALLOWED TO MEET WITH POLITICAL LEADERS BEFORE AN ELECTION TO LIST THEIR DEMANDS

GUINEA-BISSAU

IDEAS

- RETIRED POLITICIANS ESPECIALLY FORMER LEADERS SHOULD REENTER POLITICS TO BRING PEACE AND TO BOOST POPULARITY FOR A PARTY

GUINEA

IDEAS

- SMALL COUNTRIES COULD VOTE FOR THEIR JUDICIARY
- GOVERNMENTS CAN REPOSSESS ASSETS OF MINING COMPANIES IF THEY ARE FOUND TO BE PAYING BRIBES TO REBELS / SELLING WEAPONS

HAITI

QUESTIONS

- WHAT REQUESTS COULD A LEADER MAKE OF THE INTERNATIONAL COMMUNITY BEFORE THEY RETIRE
- HOW CAN THE CHURCH HELP AND REFORM PRISONERS

IDEAS

- RENTING INTERNATIONAL NGOS BY COMMUNITIES – MATCHING FUNDING ON A ONE-TO-ONE BASIS
- A SINGLE FIXED PRICE FOR ALL BUS / TRAIN JOURNEYS NO MATTER HOW LONG THE JOURNEY

HONDURAS

IDEAS

- COULD THE EU REWARD COUNTRIES FOR APPLYING HUMAN RIGHTS AND DEMOCRATIC PRINCIPLES
- PRIESTS SHOULD MOVE INTO AND LIVE AMONG POOR COMMUNITIES

HUNGARY

QUESTIONS

- HOW CAN EUROPEAN UNIVERSITIES HELP THE THIRD WORLD WHAT KIND OF PROJECTS CAN THEY COLLABARATE ON
- HOW CAN THE CHURCH BECOME RELEVANT AGAIN AND BE A FORCE FOR CHANGE AGAIN

IDEAS

- EUROPE HAS TO GO TO THE MOON
- A USIP FOR EUROPE IN GREECECOUNTRIES
- STUDENTS SHOULD BE IN SCHOOL UNTIL AN OLDER AGE BEFORE ENTERING COLLEGE

INDIA

QUESTIONS

- HOW CAN THE LEGACY OF GANDHI PROMOTE PEACE BETWEEN MUSLIMS AND HINDUS
- AS INDIA IS A BIG COUNTRY WHAT KIND OF INTERNATIONAL RESEARCH PROJECTS COULD IT WORK ON

IDEAS

- INDIA COULD SPECIALISE IN HIKING TOURS LIKE VIETNAM
- INDIA IS LARGE ENOUGH THAT IT COULD HAVE ITS OWN VERSION OF THE NOBEL PRIZES

MANTRA

- CAMPAIGN AGAINST NUCLEAR WEAPONS – AS LONG AS ONE COUNTRY HAS NUCLEAR OTHERS WILL WANT THEM TOO

INDONESIA

QUESTIONS

- HOW CAN THE INDONESIAN GOVERNMENT USE ITS UNIVERSITIES TO IMPROVE THE ECONOMY AND WORK WITH OTHER COUNTRIES
- WHAT KIND OF ENVIRONMENTAL FEATURES BE ADAPTED TO DEVELOP INDUSTRY

IDEAS

- THE EASIEST LANGUAGE TO LEARN IS THE LANGUAGE EVERY PERSON SHOULD LEARN
- JOURNALISTS SHOULD NOT HAVE TO GO TO PRISON FOR CRITICISING A POLITICIAN – WHAT SHOULD BE INSTEAD IS ALLOWING THEM A "RIGHT OF REPLY"

IRAN

QUESTIONS

- HOW CAN PEOPLE WHO ARE NOT MUSLIM AFFIRM THE MUSLIM RELIGION
- WHAT CAN IRAN LEARN FROM OTHER EDUCATIONAL SYSTEMS TO IMPROVE THE ITS UNIVERSITY GRADUATES

IDEAS

- SET UP A CAMPUS OF SEVERAL MOSQUES TOGETHER AT A FAMOUS SITE – MUSLIMS LOVE SPENDING MONEY ON MOSQUES
- BEGIN EACH PARLIAMENTARY MEETING WITH A PRAYER
- BREAKFAST LUNCH BETWEEN POLITICIANS AND BUSINESS LEADERS FROM OTHER COUNTRIES
- ISLAM WAS CREATED TO SAVE HUMANITY

IRAQ

QUESTIONS

- HOW CAN THE MILITARY BEFRIEND THE PUBLIC AND WIN THEIR TRUST
- AT WHAT LEVEL CAN THE MEDIA CRITICISE POLITICIANS AND THE GOVERNMENT. WHAT AVENUES FOR IMPROVEMENT CAN THERE BE

IDEAS

- RESTORE IRANS BORDERS IN RETURN FOR GREATER ACCESS TO THE SEA
- THE ARMY SHOULD ALLOW MILITARY HOSPITALS TO BE USED BY THE PUBLIC

IRELAND

QUESTIONS

- HOW CAN OTHER COUNTRIES ASSIST IRELAND IN IMPROVING ITS TELEVISION AND FILM INDUSTRY
- LOW ALCOHOL DRINKS FOR STUDENTS – WHAT DO YOU THINK

IDEAS

- POLICE EMBASSIES FOR SEVERAL AFRICAN COUNTRIES
- THERE SHOULD BE NO COMPULSORY SUBJECTS IN SCHOOL – KIDS WOULD LEARN MORE IF THEY DID NOT HAVE TO STUDY ENGLISH
- RE FISH-FARMING SPREADING CHEMICALS IS DAMAGING THE ENVIRONMENT – USE STRAW INSTEAD. THIS COULD BE USED TO CLEAN UP RIVERS
- IRELAND SHOULD ESTABLISH CULTURAL CENTERS IN OTHER COUNTRIES – GAA ¦ LANGUAGE ¦ IRISH DANCING ¦ ST PATRICK'S DAY WHEREVER THERE ARE LARGE NUMBERS OF DIASPORA
- IRELAND COULD DEVELOP A BUSINESS OUT OF MEDICALL CARE FOR FOREIGNERS
- A GOOD IDEA FOR TOURISM IS HOLDING SHELTERED MARKETS AT NIGHT

ISRAEL

QUESTIONS

- WHAT ASPECTS OF FAITH CAN JEWS AND MUSLIMS AGREE TO INTERPRET ON
- WHAT KIND OF ACTIONS CAN MUSLIM NATIONS TAKE TO REACH OUT TO JEWS
- WHAT KIND OF QUOTES HAVE MUSLIM AND JEWISH LEADERS MADE RE: PEACE

IDEAS

- ISRAEL COULD ESTABLISH A LEADING INTERNATIONAL ISLAMIC CULTURAL CENTER WITH ASSISTANCE FROM THE AL-AZHAR UNIVERSITY [EGYPT] SOMEWHERE IN JERUSALEM
- ALLOW A REALLY BIG MOSQUE TO BE BUILT IN JERUSALEM

- ACKNOWLEDGE THE GREATNESS OF THEIR RELIGION | TALK ABOUT THE HOLOCAUST TO THEM
- CHESS COMPETITIONS BETWEEN ISRAEL AND PALESTINE

ITALY

IDEAS

- RE FIGHTING THE MAFIA – A SUSPICIOUS LOOK / A UNIFORMED POLICE OFFICER ESPECIALLY IF THERE IS SOMEONE ELSE WITH THEM CAN FREAK THEM OUT.
- THE ITALIAN POLICE COULD RECRUIT WOMEN, THE ELDERLY, YOUNG PEOPLE AND ESPECIALLY THOSE WHO HAVE SUFFERED INTO THEIR UNOFFICIAL POLICE

IVORY COAST

QUESTIONS

- HOW CAN FRANCE ASSIST ITS AFRICAN FRIENDS RE EMPLOYMENT AND EDUCATION
- AFRICAN BRAND NAME PRODUCTS ARE VERY LIMITED WHAT CAN BE DONE TO CHANGE THIS

IDEAS

- FORMER COLONIAL POWERS SHOULD SEEK TO MAKE "HISTORICAL AMENDS" WITH AFRICAN NATIONS
- WOULD FRANCE ACCEPT MILITARY LEADERS / DICTATORS INTO ITS COUNTRY IN EXCHANGE FOR DEMOCRACY – THEY WORK FOR A TERM AND THEN LEAVE
- WOULD THE FRENCH GOVERNMENT ESTABLISH UNIVERSITY CAMPUSES IN FRENCH-SPEAKING NATIONS IN AFRICA
- A FRENCH COMMONWEALTH

JAMAICA

QUESTIONS

- HOW CAN NGOS FIGHT DRUGS
- GANGLAND MEMBERS IN PRISONS SHOULD RECORD VIDEOS ABOUT THEIR REGRETS. HOW THEY FEEL ABOUT THEIR LIVES AND HOW THEY PLAN TO MAKE AMENDS

JAPAN

QUESTIONS

- HOW CAN JAPAN WORK TO END NUCLEAR WEAPONS
- WHAT CAN BE DRAWN FROM JAPANS EXPERIENCE OF NUCLEAR BOMBS TO PREVENT THE SPREAD OF NUCLEAR WEAPONS IN THE WORLD

IDEAS

- REWARD COUNTRIES THAT HAVE CONTRIBUTED THE MOST TO AN INTERNATIONAL ORGANIZATION
- JAPAN SHOULD BAN WHALE FISHING – THEY ARE PROBABLY SENTIENT CREATURES AS ARE DOLPHINS

- RE: TERRITORIAL RIGHTS OVER DISPUTED ISLANDS – CAN AGREE THAT LAND BELONGS TO ONE COUNTRY AND THE OTHER COUNTRY CONTROLS FISHING RIGHTS AROUND THE ISLAND
- JAPAN SHOULD REWARD COUNTRIES FOR GIVING UP NUCLEAR WEAPONS
- THIS COUNTRY SHOULD TRY TO BUILD REALLY CHEAP CARS FOR THE THIRD WORLD
- HEAVY PLASTICS – JAPAN COULD WORK WITH NORTHERN IRELAND ON DOING RESEARCH INTO THIS
- JAPANESE BUSINESSES COULD SET UP RESEARCH CENTRES IN OTHER COUNTRIES INCLUDING NORTHERN IRELAND

MANTRA

- PLAY TO YOUR STRENGHTS – PRODUCE CHEAP SUBSIDISED GAMES FOR CHILDREN IN POOR COUNTRIES

JORDAN

QUESTIONS

- HOW CAN THE ROYAL FAMILY PROMOTE ITS COUNTRY
- HOW CAN MUSLIMS WORK TOGETHER TO PROMOTE TOURISM
- HOW CAN BUSINESSES PERSUADE ATTACKERS TO GIVE UP VIOLENCE

IDEAS

- A PEER REVIEW ORGANISATION – LOCATED IN JORDAN WITH BASES IN EVERY MUSLIM COUNTRY IT HAS ITS OWN NEWSPAPER / NEWSLETTER– THIS ORGANISATION SHOULD BE ABLE TO PUBLISH THESE IN ALL MUSLIM COUNTRIES. THIS RIGHT MUST BE COMPULSORY TO BE A MEMBER OF THE OIC

KAZAKHISTAN

IDEAS

- MUSLIM ARTISTS / SINGERS FROM THE WEST VISITING MUSLIM COUNTRIES TELLING PEOPLE THERE HOW THEY ARE BEING TREATED IN THE WEST
- MUSLIM AUTHORS SHOULD WORK ON PRODUCING CHILDRENS STORIES ABOUT MOHAMMED
- ALL MUSLIM COUNTRIES SHOULD ALLOW PROTESTS AT LEAST OUTSIDE CITIES

KENYA

QUESTIONS

- KENYA NEEDS TO BROADEN ITS TOURISM BASE HOW CAN OTHERS HELP THEM
- WHO CAN HELP BRING PEACE HERE. WHAT ISSUES DOES KENYA FACE
- KENYA NEEDS TO DIVERSIFY ITS PRODUCT BASE - WHAT PRODUCTS COULD IT EXPAND INTO

KOREA, NORTH

IDEAS

- BREAK THE RULES – ASK MYANMAR [THEY MAY BE YOUR FRIEND] TO ASSIST IN REPLICATING THE PROCESSES THEY WENT THROUGH TO CHANGE THEIR POLITICAL SYSTEM

- THIS COUNTRY NEEDS TO ESTABLISH A BUFFER ZONE WITH SOUTH KOREA – THIS COUNTRY WOULD PROBABLY NOT FAVOR MILITARY TROOPS BUT THE RED CROSS COULD ESTABLISH A BUFFER ZONE THEMSELVES
- MILITARY BASES ALLOWING THEIR MEDICAL FACILITIES TO BE USED BY LOCAL COMMUNITIES
- A WRITERS COLLEGE FOR THE COUNTRY – DRAW IN WRITERS FROM ALL OVER THE WORLD
- PROVIDED THEY ALLOW IN IAEA MEMBERS THEY SHOULD BE ALLOWED TO BUILD AND OR LAUNCH SATELITES
- NORTH KOREA SHOULD RECEIVE NEW TECHNOLOGIES FOR ITS NUCLEAR INDUSTRY
- THIS COUNTRY COULD ALLOW INDIVIDUALS RATHER THAN POLITICAL PARTIES TO ENTER PARLIAMENT
- LEARN AND ESTABLISH PROCEDURES FOR SHARING RESOURCES ON RIVER BOUNDARIES – I AM THINKING SPECIFICALLY OF THE ITAIPU DAM BETWEEN BRAZIL AND PARAGUAY
- ALLOW BUDDHISTS INTO NORTH KOREA – BUDDHISTS ARE VERY BRAVE AND CHARITABLE – I DO NOT THINK THEY WOULD QUESTION POLITICS
- DOES NORTH KOREA WANT TO COPY THE EXAMPLE OF CHINA WHEN IT COMES TO REFORMING POLITICS
- WHEN VISITING SOUTH KOREA FOR PEACE TALKS – BRING YOUR FAMILY ALONG WITH YOU – YOU BOTH SPEAK THE SAME LANGUAGE
- NORTH KOREA SHOULD SELL ITS ROCKETS TO OTHER NATIONS WITH SPACE AGENCIES – RUSSIA DID THIS FOR THE USA
- SKI RESORTS FOR TOURISTS – IT IS OKAY TO HAVE "MINDERS" – BUT THESE PEOPLE SHOULD BE ABLE TO SPEAK ENGLISH
- THIS COUNTRY SHOULD ENCOURAGE DEBATES AMONG STUDENTS IN NATIONAL AND LOCAL COMPETITIONS – THE PRESIDENT KIM YONG UN MUST PROMISE THAT THESE DEBATES WOULD BE UNCENSORED
- NORTH KOREA COULD SPECIALISE IN PRODUCING SUBMARINES AND HELICOPTERS AS THEY HAVE A LARGE MILITARY

KOREA, SOUTH

QUESTIONS

- HOW CAN THE BORDER BETWEEN NORTH AND SOUTH KOREA BE TRANSFORMED
- WHAT KIND OF CULTURAL EXCHANGES BE MADE BETWEEN THE TWO KOREAS

IDEAS

- EXCHANGE OF BOOKS WRITTEN BY KOREAN AUTHORS NORTH AND SOUTH
- EXCHANGING A CITY BETWEEN THE TWO KOREAS

KOSOVO

QUESTIONS

- HOW CAN KOSOVO DEAL WITH THE ISSUE OF IDENTITY
- WHAT CAN BE DONE TO MAKE A COUNTRY YIELD TO INTERNATIONAL PRESSURE ON AN ISSUE
- WHAT CAN A DIASPORA DO TO HELP THEIR HOME COUNTRY
- HOW CAN FAMILIES FROM ACROSS THE DIVIDE HELP END ETHNIC HOSTILITIES

IDEAS

- PRIESTS OTHER RELIGIOUS LEADERS SHOULD LIST THE PROBLEMS MINORITIES ARE FACING IN THEIR COMMUNITY
- SENIOR POLICE OFFICERS SHOULD ENSURE THE INTEGRITY OF THEIR JUNIOR POLICE MEMBERS IN EACH STATION
- FORMER POLITICAL LEADERS SHOULD MEET AND SHARE IDEAS ON PEACEMAKING / PEACE IDEAS
- A CONFIDENCE BUILDING MEASURE ALLOW LEADERS OF CONFLICT COUNTRIES TO TAKE SEATS ON THE SECURITY COUNCIL SUCH AS SYRIA MAY HELP BRING PEACE
- ANTICIPATE PROBLEMS CONFLICT COUNTRIES ARE LIABLE TO EXPERIENCE OR THAT MAY HAPPEN AGAIN
- TRIPLE VOTING FOR MINORITIES
- BUSINESSES SHOULD INVEST IN UNIVERSITIES
- RADIO LICENCES ARE ONLY FOR A SET NUMBER OF YEARS – COMPETING GROUPS SHOULD PROVIDE PORTFOLIOS OF THE TYPE OF PROGRAMMING THEY INTEND TO PRODUCE

KUWAIT

QUESTIONS

- HOW CAN ISLAM SAVE THE WORLD
- SOME MUSLIM COUNTRIES ARE MONARCHIES HOW CAN THEY PROMOTE OPENNESS AND EMPOWER PEOPLE IN FOREIGNERS

IDEAS

- INTERNATIONAL SCHOOLS FOR FOREIGNERS
- BIG BUILDINGS ARE MECCAS FOR FINANCIAL BUSINESSES
- WHAT WOULD YOU TRADE WITH IRAQ FOR THEM TO HAVE A LARGER COASTLINE – MORE ACCESS TO THE SEA FOR SHIPPING

KYRGYZSTAN

QUESTIONS

- HOW CAN INTERNATIONAL MEDIA PROMOTE OPENNESS IN ASIA
- WHAT KIND OF PEER MECHANISMS COULD THE INTERNATIONAL APPLY TO CENTRAL AASIA

IDEAS

- A SMALL NATIONS ALLIANCE WITH OTHER SMALL NATIONS UNDER TEN MIIDEAS
- SINCE THE EU RESTRICTS PLANES FROM THIS COUNTRY ENTERING ITS SPACE - MAYBE THE EU SET UP A BASE WITHIN THIS COUNTRY AND VET PLANES ON AN INDIVIDUAL BASIS

LAOS

QUESTIONS

- HOW CAN POLITICIANS FROM OTHER COUNTRIES PROMOTE HUMAN RIGHTS
- WHO DO CONSERVATIVE COUNTRIES RESPECT - WHO WILL THEY LISTEN TO ACCEPT CRITICISM FROM

- POLITICIANS VISITING POLITICAL PRISONERS IN OTHER COUNTRIES

LATVIA

IDEAS

- APOLOGISING FOR SOMETHING EVEN IF YOU HAVE DONE NOTHING WRONG - SIMPLY BECAUSE YOU ARE NOT HAPPY ABOUT THE WAY THINGS TURNED OUT AND SAY THIS.
- THERE SHOULD BE INVESTIGATION INTO WHAT PRECURSORS THERE ARE FOR A COUP, WHY IT HAPPENS AND HOW IT IS DEALT WITH AND HOW IT CAN BE DEALT WITH IN THE FUTURE

LEBANON

QUESTIONS

- HOW CAN A GOVERNMENT EMPOWER ITS MINORITIES
- COULD MUSLIMS REACH OUT TO CHRISTIANS - WHAT KIND OF RELIGIOUS PRACTICES FROM OTHER RELIGIONS COULD THEY ADOPT
- HOW CAN SMALL COUNTRIES WORK TOGETHER TO PROMOTE HUMAN RIGHTS

IDEAS

- RESTORING THE GRAVE YARDS OF OTHER RELIGIOUS GROUPS – MAKING AMENDS
- REACHING OUT TO MUSLIMS - MUSLIMS KNOW THEIR HISTORY - YOU COULD ASK THEM HAVE YOU HEARD OF SAINT FRANCIS ASSISI
- PEOPLE SHOULD BE ABLE TO DECIDE FOR THEMSELVES WHERE THEY PURSUE JUSTICE TRIBAL / RELIGIOUS / POLITICAL / CIVIC
- THE MANTRA FOR ISLAM COULD BE "THE MESSAGE REMAINS THE SAME BUT THE METHOD OF PREACHING IT CHANGES WITH THE TIME". TAKE FOR EXAMPLE SHARIA LAW – MOHAMMAD DID NOT CREATE THIS
- USING THE D'HONDT METHOD OF GOVERNANCE WHICH IS ALSO USED IN NORTHERN IRELAND

LESOTHO

IDEAS

- WOULD SOUTH AFRICA PROVIDE A LAND ROUTE FOR LESOTHO TO THE COAST – FRIENDS DO THINGS FOR EACH OTHER FOR FREE
- AN INDOOR CONSERVATORY FOR PLANTS – COULD SELL THESE AT HIGH PRICES TO GARDENERS. LESOTHO COULD SET UP A NETWORK OF SHOPS IN THE WEST TO SELL PLANTS FROM AFRICA
- A MILITARY PEACE CORPS – SOLDIERS CAN TAKE LEAVE FOR 1 – 2 YEARS AND HELP NGOS IN OTHER POOR COUNTRIES OR THEIR OWN COUNTRY

LIBERIA

QUESTIONS

- HOW CAN POLICE GAIN THE TRUST OF THE PUBLIC - WHAT HAVE OTHER POLICE FORCES IN THE WORLD DONE

Comment []:

IDEAS

- EACH RELIGION SHOULD CHECK OUT THE COMPETITION AND ADOPT THEIR PRACTICES – A BIG ONE WOULD BE RECOGNISING THE POPE – IN LEBANON THE MARONITE CHURCH RECOGNISES THE POPE
- A ZO0 RATHER THAN A SAFARI WOULD ATTRACT MORE VISITORS
- THE PRESIDENT IS APPOINTED BY JUDICIARY
- POLICE SHOULD BE UNARMED
- THE SECRET SERVICE SHOULD COME FROM THE POLICE

LIBYA

QUESTION

- WHAT AGENCIES CAN LIBYA WORK WITH TO ACHIEVE PEACE IN THE WORLD
- WHAT KIND OF ADMISSIONS OF GUILT FOR WRONG-DOINGS COULD LIBYA MAKE

IDEAS

- "ROOM FOR IMPROVEMENT" – HUMAN RIGHTS / DEMOCRACY – INTERNATIONAL AGENCIES SUCH AS MEDICINES SAN FRONTIERS
- IF YOU KEEP FIGHTING SIN FOR LONG ENOUGH YOU WILL DO GREAT THINGS
- SOMETIMES YOU NEED TO APPLY "FRONT-LOADING" FOR COUNTRIES YOU THINK WILL NOT CHANGE
- A PEACE COLLEGE FUNDED BY THE UN – THE UN SHOULD SET UP THESE COLLEGES ALL OVER THE WORLD

LITHUANIA

QUESTIONS

- WHAT KIND OF POLITICS SPREADS OVER BORDERS
- HOW CAN NATURE BE USED TO PROMOTE TOURISM

IDEAS

- DISSIDENTS SHOULD BE ALLOWED TO LEAVE THE COUNTRY RATHER THAN BEING IMPRISONED
- MEMBERS OF THE EU CAN RUN FOR ELECTION IN OTHER EU COUNTRIES

LUXEMBOURG

IDEAS

- A PROFESSIONAL INTERNATIONAL NGO FOR PRODUCING FLAGS AND ANTHEMS
- BRAND-NAMING UNIVERSITIES TO ATTRACT STUDENTS EG MICHELANGELO COLLEGE, KHADIJA COLLEGE

MACEDONIA

IDEAS

- ITALY WHICH IS A RICHER COUNTRY COULD PROVIDE SCHOLARSHIPS TO STUDENTS FROM MACEDONIA – FULL TERMS [FOUR YEARS] – THEY DO HOWEVER HAVE TO STATE WHETHER THEY PLAN TO STAY IN THE COUNTRY AFTER THEIR EDUCATION
- THE UN CAN TAKE COUNTRIES TO COURT

MADAGASGAR

QUESTIONS

- WHAT KIND OF ACTIVITIES CAN THE CHURCH TAKE ON TO HELP AFRICAN COUNTRIES. BASED ON ACTIVITIES THEY ARE NOT YET INVOLVED IN
- HOW CAN RETIRED POLITICIANS HELP BRING PEACE TO THEIR COUNTRY
- WHAT KIND OF EXPERIENCE DOES THE INTERNATIONAL COMMUNITY HAVE IN RADIO BROADCASTING FOR POOR COUNTRIES

IDEAS

- EDUCATION IN THE ENGLISH LANGAUGE FOR ALL STUDENTS FROM AN EARLY AGE
- POLITICIANS IN AFRICA NEED TO LEARN TO ASK FOR HELP FROM DEVELOPED NATIONS
- THERE SHOULD BE MORE SPENDING ON POLICE THAN ON THE MILITARY

MALAWI

QUESTIONS

- WHAT KIND OF INNOVATIVE APPROACHES BE USED TO PROVIDE HEALTHCARE

IDEAS

- AFRICAN JUDUCIARY TRAINED IN THE UK
- A RESEARCH CENTER FOR AFRICAN DISEASES – THE UK GOVERNMENT COULD SPONSOR ONE OF THEIR PHARMACEUTICAL BUSINESSES TO ESTABLISH SUCH A CENTER THERE
- A SMALL MONETARY REWARD TO PARENTS FOR SENDING THEIR CHILDREN TO SCHOOL

MALAYSIA

QUESTIONS

- HOW CAN AGENCIES REACH OUT TO MUSLIMS AND AFFIRM THE ISLAMIC FAITH

IDEAS

- REGIONAL PEACE CENTER FOR NEIGHBOURING COUNTRIES – NOT POLITICIANS BUT HAVE POWER TO IMPLEMENT FOREIGN POLICY – FOREIGN POLICY IS NOW AN NGO BUSINESS
- THE SPRATLY ISLANDS DISPUTES COULD BE RESOLVED UNDER THE FOLLOWING CRITERIA – TERRITORY / RESOURCES / FISHING RIGHTS / CONTIGUITY
- SELLING A SMALL AMOUNT OF LAND ON THE COAST TO ANOTHER COUNTRY FOR THEM TO ESTABLISH A TRADING POST – COULD HELP DEVELOP THEIR ECONOMY
- I RECKON FOOD CROPS THAT GROW IN COOLER CLIMATES SUCH AS IRELAND WOULD GROW EVEN MORE PROLIFICALLY IN THIS COUNTRY
- AN INDEPENDENT MEDIA ON THE INTERNET AND NEWSPAPERS SUPPORTED BY FREELANCE JOURNALISTS – LIKE "COMMON DREAMS" IN THE USA

MALI

QUESTIONS

- HOW CAN WOMEN BRIDGE THE GAPS BETEWEEN ETHNIC GROUPS
- HOW CAN TECHNOLOGY BE USED TO PROMOTE PEACE
- WHAT KIND OF CLOTHES COULD MUSLIM NATÍONS IN AFRICA PROMOTE IN THE WEST

IDEAS

- MUSLIM ATTACKERS COULD APOLOGISE FOR CIVILIAN CASUALTIES
- RESEARCH INTO TRIBAL CURES IN AFRICA
- WOMEN, STUDENTS, RELIGIOUS AND NGOS SHOULD BE ALLOWED TO PROTEST
- DOCTORS ACROSS AFRICA SHOULD WORK TO END FEMALE GENITAL MUTILATION AS IT CAUSES EXTREME PAIN TO WOMEN IN CHILDBIRTH

MALTA

QUESTIONS

- HOW CAN EU SCIENTIFIC AGENCIES SUCH AS THE ESA HELP POOR AFRICAN COUNTRIES
- WHAT CAN BE LEARNED ABOUT TOURISM FROM THE EXAMPLE OF IRELAND AND NORTHERN IRELAND

IDEAS

- POLITICAL PARTIES SHOULD HAVE NAMES THAT MEAN SOMETHING – THEIR MANTRA
- THE VATICAN SHOULD ADOPT CITIES ALL OVER THE WORLD. THIS WOULD BE ESPECIALLY GOOD FOR AFRICA. LEGALLY CONTROLLED BY THE VATICAN

MAURITANIA

QUESTIONS

- WITHDRAWING FROM THE FORMER WESTERN SAHARA – RESTORING THEIR INDEPENDENCE
- WHO TAKES RESPONSIBILITY FOR NEGOTIATIONS - YOU NEED TO BREAK THE RULES AND EMPLOY PEOPLE YOU DID NOT PLAN TO ON INCLUDING

IDEAS

- RELIGIOUS LEADERS FROM OTHER MUSLIM COUNTRIES VISITING A LEADER AND BERATING THEM ON THEIR LACK OF FREEDOM

MEXICO

IDEAS

- TRIBAL GROUPS SHOULD HAVE THEIR OWN IMAGE OF JESUS AND MARY

MOLDOVA

IDEAS

- MOLDOVA AGREES TO ACCEPT THE ROUBLE IN RETURN FOR PEACE AGREEMENT WITH TRANSNISTRIA
- A NATIONAL LIBRARY IN BOTH TRANSNISTRIA AND MOLDOVA

- RUSSIA COULD BUY LAND FROM MOLDOVA FOR TRANSNISTRIA AS LONG AS TRANSNISTRIA REMAINS PART OF M0LDOVA

MONGOLIA

QUESTIONS

- WHAT KIND OF GOOD WORKS CAN BUDDHISTS DO FOR THEIR COUNTRY
- CAN YOU LIST EXAMPLES OF GOOD WORKS DONE BY BUDDHISTS AROUND THE WORLD

IDEAS

- HARVESTING THE PEAT – IRELAND ASSISTS THEM IN DEVELOPING THIS – THERE IS A HUGE MARKET IN CHINA FOR PEAT
- POINT OUT SILENCE BRINGS YOU CLOSER TO GOD

MONTENEGRO

QUESTIONS

- WHAT KIND OF POLITICAL POWERS CAN AN ETHNIC REGION HAVE. HOW CAN YOU GIVE THEM INFLUENCE
- WHAT KIND OF CULTURAL AND SOCIAL POWERS COULD BE ENACTED TO HELP DIFFERENT ETHNIC GROUPS FIND COMMON GROUND

IDEAS

- A SINGLE PURPOSE CONSULATE EG THIRD WORLD AID / PEACE / CORRUPTION
- FORMER YUGOSLAV COUNTRIES SHOULD READOPT PLACENAMES USED DURING COMMUNIST RULE

MOROCCO

QUESTIONS

- TOO MANY PEOPLE THINK THEY CAN ISSUE A FATWA - WHAT KIND OF CRITERIA COULD ALL MUSLIM COUNTRIES APPLY TO REGULATE THIS

IDEAS

- MILITARY EXERCISES FOR MORROCCO AND NATO MEMBERSHIP IN RETURN FOR RESTORING WESTERN SAHARA

MOZAMBIQUE

QUESTIONS

- HOW CAN THIS COUNTRY DEVELOP FRIENDSHIPS WITH THE WEST
- WHAT KIND OF NGOS COULD AFRICAN NATIONS FOSTER TO HELP THEMSELVES

IDEAS

- AN INTERNATIONAL FBI FOR PROTECTION OF POLITICAL LEADERS - IT HAS TO BE A POLICE AGENCY THAT HAS A LOT OF INTEGRITY - SMALL NATIONS COUKD DO THIS
- CHURCHES SHOULD BE OPEN TO TAKING IN THE POOR – THEY SHOULD BE CENTERS FOR MEDICINE AND WATER AND FOOD RESERVES

- NEWSPAPERS CAN BE POSTED ON WALLS

MYANMAR

QUESTIONS

- WHAT KIND OF ACTIVITIES COULD RELIGIOUS ORGANISATIONS PURSUE FOR THOSE LIVING ON THE MARGINS
- WHEN A COUNTRY MOVES FROM A DICTATORSHIP TO DEMOCRACY WHAT KIND OF RESPONSIBILITIES WOULD THE MILITARY HAVE
- WHEN POLITICIANS VISIT A CONSERVATIVE COUNTRY WHAT COULD THEY ACHIEVE - WHAT CAN BE LEARNED FROM PAST EXAMPLES
- WHAT KIND OF ACCESS COULD FOREIGN POLITICIANS HAVE OVER LOCAL MEDIA

IDEAS

- ENGLISH SPEAKING TV STATIONS AND ENGLISH LANGUAGE NEWSPAPERS
- DO MUSLIMS WANT TO CREATE "RETREATS" - SIMILAR TO THE CATHOLIC CHURCH FOR SCHOOL STUDENTS
- A SINGLE GOVERNMENT IN THE THIRD WORLD WILL NOT ACHIEVE EVERYTHING – IT SHOULD PRIORITIZE ONE OR TWO GOALS
- ALLOWING PROTESTS BUT OUTSIDE CITIES
- THE MANTRA FOR PEOPLE WHO HAVE DONE WRONG IS MAKING AMENDS AND NOT PUNISHMENTS OR TRADE SANCTIONS

NAMIBIA

IDEAS

- AN AU TENDERING AGENCY FOR SELECTING BUSINESSES FOR INVESTMENTS IN AN AFRICAN COUNTRY
- NO TAXES ON FOOD / UNIFORMS AND SCHOOL BOOKS
- RICH FARMERS SHOULD ALLOW POOR PEASANTS TO LIVE ON THEIR LAND FOR FREE IF THEY ARE CLOSE TO CITIES AND TOWNS. THERE SHOULD BE A LAW ABOUT THIS. IT MAY REDUCE THE AMOUNT OF POOR PEOPLE FLOODING INTO CITIES.

NEPAL

QUESTIONS

- HOW CAN FAMOUS PEOPLE PROMOTE THEIR COUNTRY ABROAD
- WHAT KIND OF PREPARATIONS CAN NEGOTIATORS MAKE BEFORE THEY MEET WITH EACH OTHER

IDEAS

- A MEDIATOR SHOULD BE ALLOWED CRITICISE LACK OF IMPLEMENTATION OF A PEACE PROCESS – "NAME AND SHAME"
- DO NOT TRY TO PROVIDE A COMPLETE PEACE AGREEMENT PEOPLE NEED TO MAKE DECISIONS FOR THEMSELVES TO OWN A PEACE PROCESS

NETHERLANDS

- HOW AND WHAT KIND OF VALUES COULD THE EU SPREAD TO OTHER PARTS OF THE WORLD
- WHAT KIND OF POLITICAL POWERS COULD THE UN BE GIVEN WITHIN A COUNTRY

IDEAS

- A LEADER TAKING THE RELIGION OF A MINORITY TO HELP BRING PEACE
- THE ROYAL FAMILY SHOULD PRACTICE THEIR FAITH ACTIVELY – AN EXAMPLE TO OTHERS

NEW ZEALAND

IDEAS

- A TOURISM IDEA WOULD BE TO CREATE A PLANETARIUM IN AUCKLAND

NICARAGUA

QUESTIONS

- WHAT QUALITIES MAKE FOR THE BEST POLICE OFFICERS
- HOW CAN THE DEVELOPED WORLD HELP LATIN AMERICA IN THE FIELDS OF SCIENCE AND TECHNOLOGY

IDEAS

- THE CHURCH SHOULD SAY THEY WANT THEIR COMMUNITIES TO BE PEACE ZONES WITH NEITHER SIDES MILITARY PRESENT – PRIESTS SHOULD LIST BY NAME THE DAILY DEATH TOLL
- BUILDING HELICOPTERS FOR LATIN AMERICA – A MILITARY AGENCY SHOULD DO THIS SUCH AS BRAZIL

NIGER

QUESTIONS

- WHAT CAN BE DONE TO PERSUADE BOKO HARAM TO LEAVE THE NATIONS SURROUNDINGS NIGERIA
- WHAT CAN BE DONE BY CIVIL SOCIETY TO END A DICTATORSHIP

IDEAS

- THE INTERNATIONAL COMMUNITY SHOULD PRIORITIZE FREEDOM OF PRESS IN THE WORLD
- ENCOURAGE WESTERN GOVERNMENTS TO ESTABLISH MILITARY BASES IN AFRICAN COUNTRIES – COULD PREVENT COUP DETATS IN AFRICAN COUNTRY'S

NIGERIA

QUESTIONS

- HOW CAN MEDIA HELP TO LIBERALISE A COUNTRY - GIVE EXAMPLES OF THIS SUCH AS SERBIA
- HOW CAN ATTACKER GROUPS BE PERSUADED TO MAKE AMENDS - CAN YOU GIVE EXAMPLES HERE

IDEAS

- POINT OUT TO BOKO HARAM THAT CREATING A SINGLE MUSLIM STATE IN THE WORLD WOULD REQUIRE AN ENORMOUS SHEDDING OF BLOOD
- I WOULD LIKE TO POINT OUT TO BOKO HARAM THAT THE UN IS NOT TRYING TO CONVERT ISLAM NOR IS IT SEEKING POWER AND FOR THEM TO ACKNOWLEDGE THAT THE UN IS DOING A LOT OF GOOD IN THE WORLD
- BROADCAST FRIDAY MASS ON TELEVISION FROM A DIFFERENT MOSQUE EVERY WEEK

MANTRA

- RE ISLAM – THE MESSAGE REMAINS THE SAME BUT THE MEANS OF CONVEYING IT CHANGES WITH THE TIMES. AN EXAMPLE OF THIS IS THAT SHARIA LAW WAS NOT CREATED BY MOHAMMAD

NORTHERN IRELAND

QUESTIONS

- WHAT CAN RELIGIOUS GROUPS DO TO PROMOTE PEACE WITHIN COMMUNITIES
- COULD RELIGIOUS GROUPS BEFRIEND POLITICIANS FROM ALL SIDES
- HOW CAN WOMEN REACH OUT TO OTHER WOMEN ON THE SAME STREET
- HOW CAN RELIGIOUS SYMBOLS PRESERVE COMMUNITIES
- WHAT CAN BE DONE TO PROMOTE INDEPENDENT IN NI
- ELDERLY PEOPLE ARE USUALLY THE LAST PEOPLE TO LEAVE A COMMUNITY - HOW CAN THEY ENCOURAGE THE YOUNGER GENERATION TO RETURN

IDEAS

- COULD OTHER CHRISTIANS ACCEPT THE POPE AS "SYMBOLIC LEADER" OF ALL CHRISTIANS. THE POPE COULD DESCRIBE PROTESTANT RELIGIONS AS PART OF THE FAMILY AND ACCEPT THAT GOD WORKS WITH THEM JUST AS MUCH AS WITH CATHOLICS
- PROTESTANTS NEED TO ADOPT THE PRINCIPLE OF MARY
- PRIESTS AND REVERENDS SHOULD ATTEND EACH OTHERS CHURCHES AND CELEBRATE MASS IN THEIR FORMAT TOGETHER
- EVERYONE THINKS THAT YOU SHOULD INVEST IN THE YOUNGER GENERATION TO BRING PEACE. THE REALITY IS THAT CONFLICT SOCIETIES ARE PEER DRIVEN - YOUNG PEOPLE WILL FOLLOW THE LEAD OF THEIR PEERS
- A SAMPLE BROADCAST OF PEACE NEGOTIATIONS BETWEEN THE VARIOUS POLITICAL PARTIES
- PEOPLE APPRECIATE OTHERS SAYING THEY HAVE HEARD OF SOMEONE FROM THAT GROUP. AN EXAMPLE WOULD BE SERBIA - HAVE YOU HEARD OF ST. LAZAR A FAMOUS SAINT FOR SERBIA
- POLITICIANS CAN MAKE THE FOLLOWING STATEMENT ABOUT PEOPLE FROM EACH OTHERS RELIGIONS - MAYBE THEY WERE SAINTS MAYBE THEY WERE NOT BUT WE DO ACCEPT THEY WERE REALLY GOOD PEOPLE
- CHANGE NAMES OF COMMUNITIES TO REALLY GOOD PEOPLE
- IF THIS WERE YOUR LAST DAY ON EARTH WHAT WOULD YOU DO
- A WOMANS NIGHT ONLY ON THE TOWN
- GERRY ADAMS WALKING AT THE FRONT OF AN ORANGE PARADE - WHATEVER THE SITUATION IN NI IS YOU HAVE TO LIVE WITH EACH OTHER
- ACTUAL PRIESTS / NUNS SHOULD SPEAK ON CITY STREETS AND NOT LEAVE THIS TO MINORITY RELIGIONS

- COULD OTHER COUNTRIES SET UP ENCLAVES IN NORTHERN IRELAND -'OWNED BY THEM. NI COULD BENEFIT ECONOMICALLY FROM THIS
- A COMMON HISTORY FOR NI BASED ON REALLY GOOD PEOPLE / UNSUNG HEROES
- ALLOW CHILDREN TO STAY UP LATER IN PUBS WITH YOUR PARENTS

NORWAY

QUESTIONS

- HOW CAN NORWAY PARTICIPATE IN EU INSTITUTIONS

IDEAS

- SOMEONE NEEDS TO WRITE DOWN THE FOLK STORIES OF PAST GENERATIONS
- INTRODUCE YOUR CULTURE TO OTHER COUNTRIES IN ENGLISH OR OTHER LOCAL LANGUAGES
- RELIGIOUS CHURCHES OFFERING COUNSELLING SHOULD NOT TRY TO CONVERT PEOPLE WHO COME TO THEM

MANTRA

- MUST SUPPORT PEACEMAKERS AROUND THE WORLD

OMAN

QUESTIONS

- HOW CAN MUSLIM UNIVERSITIES PROMOTE REALLY GOOD PEOPLE IN SOCIETY
- WHAT KIND OF

IDEAS

- RESTORATION OF CULTURAL / HISTORICAL / RELIGIOUS SITES – SAUDI ARABIA FINANCES THIS FOR BOTH SUNNIS AND SHIAS AND CHRISTIANS AND JEWS
- COULD INTERNATIONAL ORGANIZATIONS SUCH AS THE IAEA TAKE DRESPONSIBILITY FOR DEALING WITH RESTRICTED COUNTRIES INSTEAD OF GOVERNMENTS
- TRACE THEIR ANCESTRY BACK TO MOHAMMAD – SHOULD BE TREATED AS RESPECTED PEOPLE
- BREAK THE RULES THERE SHOULD BE MOVIES AND CHILDREN'S STORIES ABOUT MOHAMMAD - YOU ALREADY HAVE BOOKS ABOUT MOHAMMED AND KHADIJA
- ALLOW LEADERS FROM UNPOPULAR COUNTRIES TO SPEAK BEFORE THE UN
- JUST LIKE ISLAM DURING RAMADAN OTHER COUNTRIES SHOULD RELEASE PRISONERS EACH YEAR

PAKISTAN

QUESTIONS

- HOW CAN A COUNTRY FILTER OUT A CAPABLE PERSON FOR POLITICS FROM THOSE WHO DO NOT HAVE THE PROPER QUALITIES
- WHAT CAN ROYALTY DO TO PROMOTE JUSTICE AND PEACE IN THE WORLD
- WHAT CAN POLITICIANS DO TO INSPIRE YOUNG CHILDREN
- WHAT ROLE MODELS WOULD MUSLIMS ACCEPT FROM OTHER RELIGIONS

IDEAS

- POWER PLANTS [THEY HAVE FREQUENT BROWNOUTS]
- JUVENILE PRISONERS SHOULD BE ALLOWED TO KEEP PETS
- WOULD MUSLIMS LIKE TO HAVE MONASTERIES LIVING IN THE COMMUNITY AND DEPENDING ON THE COMMUNITY
- IN PEACE NEGOTIATIONS BETWEEN PAKISTAN AND INDIA OVER KASHMIR THE FIRST LINE OF NEGOTIATIONS SHOULD BE WHAT YOU NEED AND NOT WHAT YOU WANT
- AN OBSERVER SECTION IN PARLIAMENT FOR NGOS, RELIGIOUS OTHERS
- THERE HAVE BEEN MORE FEMALE LEADERS IN ISLAM THAN CHRISTIANITY
- IMAMS / PRIESTS COULD GIVE SERMONS IN EACH OTHERS PLACES OF WORSHIP – THIS WILL HELP BRING PEACE TO THIS WORLD
- NO ONE SHOULD BE PROUD TO HAVE NUCLEAR WEAPONS. IT IS NOT A MODERN SOCIETY TO HAVE NUCLEAR WEAPONS
- MUSLIMS SHOULD BE CONCERNED WITH ISSUES IN OTHER COUNTRIES OUTSIDE OF ISLAM
- POLICE SHOULD GET THE SAME TRAINING AS THE ARMY

MANTRA

- REFORM POLITICS – TO ENTER POLITICS YOU MUST HAVE SOME SORT OF QUALIFICATION – PAKISTAN MUST WORK ON REFORM OF POLITICS AROUND THE WORLD

PALESTINE

QUESTIONS

- HOW CAN THE WEST MAKE AMENDS FOR ITS TREATMENT OF MUSLIMS
- WHAT KIND OF PERCEPTIONS DO PEOPLE HAVE OF MUSLIMS - HOW CAN THIS BE CHANGED
- PEOPLE SHOULD BE ASKED WHAT REALLY GOOD MUSLIMS THEY KNOW ABOUT
- HOW CAN PEOPLE FIND OUT ABOUT MUSLIMS

IDEAS

- A MISPERCEPTION MANY PEOPLE FEEL MOST MUSLIM WOMEN ARE ILLITERATE – IN FACT THIS IS NOT TRUE – LITERACY RATES FOR WOMEN ARE THE SAME AS IN ANY OTHER THIRD WORLD COUNTRY
- THE MAJORITY OF MUSLIMS ARE NOT ARABS. EIGHTY PERCENT OF MUSLIMS ARE NOT ARABS. THE TOP FOUR MUSLIM COUNTRIES INDONESIA, PAKISTAN, BANGLADESH AND INDIA ARE NOT ARABS
- VISIT A MOSQUE MUSLIMS WOULD APPRECIATE THIS
- BREAK THE RULES – I KNOW MUSLIMS FORBID CREATING IMAGES OF MOHAMMAD BUT MAYBE THEY COULD ALLOW YOUNG CHILDREN TO DO THIS

PANAMA

QUESTIONS

- HOW CAN GOVERNMENTS MAKE AMENDS FOR HISTORICAL WRONGS
- HOW CAN CORRUPTION BE DEALT ON A CITY-CITY BBASIS

IDEAS

- INTERNATIONAL COMMUNITY RENTS THE PANAMA CANAL – THE FOUR BASES FOR HELPING THIS AND OTHER THIRD WORLD COUNTRIES ARE POLICE / NGOs / CREDIT UNIONS AND WOMEN

- THE HEAD OF THE ARMY SHOULD BE A SENIOR POLICE OFFICER
- TRIBAL / ETHNIC GROUPS SHOULD NOT HAVE TO PAY TAXES

PAPUA NEW GUINEA

QUESTIONS

- WHAT ARE THE FIRST STEPS A RESTRICTIVE COUNTRY COULD TAKE TO OPENING UP A COUNTRY
- WHAT INSTITUTIONS ARE THERE TO HELP AND PROTECT WOMEN

IDEAS

- BUILD VILLAGES CLOSE TO TOWNS
- WHATEVER LANGUAGE WAS SPOKEN DURING COLONIAL RULE IS THE LANGUAGE THE COUNTRY SHOULD TEACH ALL PEOPLES IN A COUNTRY
- RESTRICTIVE COUNTRIES SHOULD ALLOW VOTES OF NO-CONFIDENCE IN PARLIAMENT

PARAGUAY

QUESTIONS

- HOW CAN TRIBAL AND ETHNIC GROUPS BE EDUCATED - WHERE DO YOU BEGIN HERE
- HOW CAN STUDENTS BEFRIEND INDIGENOUS INDIANS. COULD STUDENTS DEVELOP POLICY DOCUMENTS FOR TREATING THEM - WHETHER IN PEACE, HEALTH OR EDUCATION
- WHAT ARE THE FIRST PRIORITIES A GOVERNMENT SHOULD HAVE IN HELPING THE MAJORITY WHO ARE POOR
- HOW CAN NEGOTIATORS LOBBY THE INTERNATIONAL COMMUNITY TO SUPPORT A PEACE DEAL
- WHAT KIND OF RELIGIOUS PRACTICES OF TRIBAL GROUPS COULD OTHER RELIGIONS ADOPT. WHAT VALUES COULD THEY PASS ON TO THEM.

IDEAS

- APOLOGISING FOR THE DEATHS OF INDIGENOUS INDIANS POLITICAL LEADERS IN THE PAST – COMPENSATION MADE NOT TO THEIR FAMILIES INSTEAD TO THE COMMUNITIES THEY CAME FROM
- INDIAN TRIBES SAYING THEY WANT NO ARMED FORCES IN THEIR TERRITORY – AS SOON AS AN INCURSION IS MADE THE GOAL IS TO SURROUND THEM WITH LARGE NUMBERS OF UNARMED INDIANS – DONE IN COLOMBIA
- MORE MONEY SHOULD BE INVESTED IN NGOS THAN ON THE MILITARY – THAT IS MY ADVICE FOR ALL THIRD WORLD COUNTRIES – THE EU SHOULD INSIST THAT THIS HAPPENS IN RETURN FOR AID. IF THEY CAN AFFORD THIS FOR THE MILITARY THEN THEY CAN AFFORD THIS FOR NGOS
- HUMAN RIGHTS GROUPS SHOULD BE ALLOWED TO STAY IN THE COUNTRY AS LONG AS THEY AVOID DISCUSSING POLITICS
- TAXES ON UNOCCUPIED / UNCULTIVATED LAND – LARGE LANDOWNERS HAVE A HABIT OF CHOOSING CATTLE RANCHING AS THEY REQUIRE LESS LABOURERS
- CANCEL ALL DEBTS OWED BY PEASANTS – A GOVERNMENT AMNESTY

PERU

QUESTIONS

- GOD HAS NOT SUDDENLY DISAPPEARED IN THE LAST CENTURY - HE IS FOR REAL AND IS STILL ACTIVE IN THE WORLD. IF ENOUGH PEOPLE PRAY AND ARE OF GOOD INTEGRITY WHAT CAN THEY DO.
- WHAT KIND OF CONTACTS SHOULD THERE BE WITH ETHNIC TRIBES
- WHAT KIND OF RIGHTS COULD THERE BE FOR THEM

IDEAS

- MULTINATIONALS CANNOT CLAIM PATENT RIGHTS OVER INDIGENOUS PLANTS. – THERE SHOULD BE NO SUICIDE SEEDS
- I WOULD NOT TRY CONVERT INDIANS – OR MODERNIZE THEM – LEAVE THEM IN PEACE AS MUCH AS POSSIBLE

PHILIPPINES

QUESTIONS

- THE MANTRA FOR NEWS AGENCIES IS INTEGRITY - WHAT CAN BE LEARNED FROM REALLY GOOD COUNTRIES SUCH AS AUSTRALIA
- WELL KNOWN LABELS THAT WE HAVE IN SOCIETY SUCH AS STATUES - HOW CAN SUCH LABELS CONTRIBUTE TO PEACE BETWEEN PEOPLES
- HOW CAN BUSINESS CORRUPTION BE TACKLED

IDEAS

- ECONOMIC ZONES LINKED TO MUSLIM ZONES - FOR DEMARCKING TERITORIAL BOUNDARIES
- START AT GO HALF WAY WHEN CHOOSING TO RESTORE MUSLIM HOMELANDS
- JUDICIARY SHOULD BE IN CHARGE OF APPOINTING SENIOR CIVIL SERVICE MEMBERS
- BONUS SEATS FOR LARGE PARTIES
- ASK CUBA TO HELP IMPROVE HEALTHCARE IN THE COUNTRY AND REWARD THEM
- ESTABLISH CULTURAL CENTERS FOR OTHER ETHNIC GROUPS IN LARGE CITIES ESPECIALLY THE CAPITAL

POLAND

QUESTIONS

- HOW CAN THE CHURCH BECOME RELEVANT TO PEOPLE - HOW CAN THEY WORK WITH ORDINARY PEOPLE FOR PEACE AND JUSTICE
- WHAT STRATEGIES EXIST FOR DEMARCATING BORDERS BETWEEN SIDES
- HOW CAN POLICE PROMOTE PEACE IN INDIVIDUAL COMMUNITIES AND COUNTRIES

IDEAS

- THE BEST WAY TO MARKET YOURSELF IS TO SET UP LANGUAGE CENTERS IN OTHER COUNTRIES
- TRAIN POLICE TO OPERATE IN PEACEKEEPING MISSIONS
- NATIONAL AIRLINES ARE USUALLY "WHITE ELEPHANTS" TOURISM WOULD BENEFIT FROM OPEN COMPETITION

MANTRA

- YOUNG PEOPLE MUST REALISE THAT IT IS WHAT YOU PUT INTO MASS AND NOT WHAT YOU GET OUT OF IT THAT MATTERS

PORTUGAL

QUESTIONS

- HOW CAN PORTUGAL INCREASE ITS INFLUENCE IN THE WORLD - HOW HAS IT DONE SO IN THE PAST
- WHAT ARE THE PRIORITIES FOR SPREADING ITS CULTURE ABROAD
- HOW CAN FAMOUS PEOPLE PROMOTE THEIR SKILLS AND MARKET THEIR COUNTRY TO OTHERS

IDEAS

- NGOS CAN MEET WITH LEADERS OF POLITICAL PARTIES BEFORE ELECTIONS TO LIST THEIR DEMANDS AND ASK THEM QUESTIONS
- RESOLVING LAND DISPUTES – WHO HAS BEEN THERE LONGEST OVER THE LAST 100 YEARS. RESOLVING TERRITORIAL ISSUES – RESOURCES OR TERRITORY AND CONTIGUITY
- NEGOTIATIONS BASED ON WHAT YOU NEED AND NOT WHAT YOU WANT

MANTRA

- SPREAD THE WORD – RELIGIOUS VALUES

QATAR

QUESTIONS

- WHAT KIND OF CULTURAL PRACTICES – THAT ARE PRESENT IN THE WEST COULD QATAR AND OTHER MUSLIM NATIONS ADOPT
- A CRITICISM OF MUSLIM NATIONS THEY ARE TOO FOCUSED ON ONLY OTHER MUSLIM NATIONS – IN WHAT WAYS COULD THIS CHANGE
- WHAT PRECEDENTS ARE THERE IN THE KORAN THAT ARE NO LONGER PRACTICED TODAY – I WOULD REFER SPECIFICALLY TO WOMEN
- IN WHAT WAYS COULD MUSLIMS CULTURE AND RELIGION CONTRIBUTE TO TOURISM

IDEAS

- SHARIA LAW WAS NOT CREATED BY MOHAMMAD. I THINK THE PRINCIPLE THE MESSAGE REMAINS THE SAME BUT THE METHODS OF DELIVERING IT CAN CHANGE WITH THE TIMES
- MEETINGS OF PARLIAMENT SHOULD BE BROADCAST OVER RADIO AND TELEVISION
- PRAGMATISM TEACHES ME THAT IN SOME COUNTRIES POLITICS IS TOO DIVIDED – A WAY OF DEALING WITH THIS IS BY GIVING BONUS SEATS TO LARGE PARTIES
- THE BUSINESS COMMUNITY CAN APPOINT THE MINISTER FOR INDUSTRY
- THIRD WORLD COUNTRIES SHOULD BE REQUIRED TO SPEND MORE ON NGO THAN ON THE MILITARY
- LEADERS OF GOVERNMENTS SHOULD APOLOGISE EVEN IF THEY HAVE DONE NOTHING WRONG – SIMPLY BECAUSE THEY ARE UNHAPPY ABOUT THE WAY THINGS TURNED OUT

ROMANIA

QUESTIONS

- HOW CAN THE INTERNATIONAL COMMUNITY HELP INDIGENOUS NGOS – WHAT HAS BEEN DONE HERE
- GIVE EXAMPLES OF CASES IN HISTORY WHERE COUNTRIES REACHED OUT TO EACH OTHER WITHOUT LOOKING FOR ANYTHING IN RETURN

IDEAS

- SEVERAL DAYS OF HUMAN RIGHTS AND NGO ACTIVITIES IN THE CAPITAL
- FRIENDS CAN DIFFER WITH EACH OTHER AND STILL REMAIN FRIENDS
- MAKING FRIENDS – THANKING OTHER COUNTRIES FOR THEIR HELP IN THE PAST – A FINANCIAL CONTRIBUTION FOR MAKING AMENDS FOR HISTORICAL WRONGDOINGS
- FRIENDS OR POWER SHOULD BE THE MANTRA FOR EVERY COUNTRY ON EARTH

RUSSIA

QUESTIONS

- HOW CAN RUSSIA INSIST THAT THE COUNTRIES IT HELPS ARE COMPLYING WITH THE STANDARDS THEY SET FOR THEM – HUMAN RIGHT / DEMOCRACY
- HOW CAN RUSSIA ENSURE THAT COUNTRIES THAT IT ASSISTS [RE: NUCLEAR POWER] DO NOT TRY TO DEVELOP NUCLEAR WEAPONS
- WHAT FIRST STEPS COULD RUSSIA TAKE TO DEAL WITH CORRUPTION – WHAT HAVE OTHER COUNTRYS IN THE DEVELOPING WORLD DONE TO TACKLE BUSINESS CORRUPTION
- WHAT CAN OTHER POLICE FORCES DO TO ASSIST RUSSIA IN COMBATING DRUGS
- HOW SHOULD LOCAL CHURCHES DEAL WITH MINORITY RELIGIONS – COMPETE WITH THEM / WORK WITH THEM

IDEAS

- THE EU AND RUSSIA COULD SET UP A JOINT MILITARY COLLEGE WHERE? IN THE BIGGEST COUNTRY OTHER THAN RUSSIA NEAREST THE BORDER BETWEEN THE EU AND RUSSIA
- RUSSIA COULD WORK TO REPATRIATE ETHNIC CHECHENS TRANSPLANTED DURING COMMUNISM BACK TO CHECHNYA – THIS COULD HELP FOSTER PEACE THERE
- DOES RUSSIA WANT TO SET UP A POLICE EMBASSY IN IRELAND. HOPEFULLY RUSSIA COULD HAVE SENIOR POLICE OFFICERS TRAINED IN IRELAND. A GOOD WAY TO MAKE FRIENDS WITH IRELAND
- THE CHRISTIAN CHURCHES COULD DECLARE PEOPLE FROM OTHER RELIGIONS AS SAINTS. DECLARING MOHAMMAD AS A SAINT COULD HELP BRING WORLD PEACE.
- THIS COUNTRY COULD SPECIALISE IN BUILDING TRAINS – A HUGE GROWTH MARKET IN ASIAN COUNTRIES
- NATO AND RUSSIA COULD SET UP MILITARY BASES IN POOR THIRD WORLD COUNTRIES - THIS COULD HELP PREVENT COUP D'ETATS
- A CIVIL SOCIETY ASSEMBLY FOR CHECHNYA
- THE MANTRA IS "I CAN'T MAKE YOU FREE BUT I CAN MAKE YOU FEEL FREE"
- REPATRIATING CHECHENS FROM OTHER PARTS OF RUSSIA – THOSE EXPORTED DURING STALINS RULE
- A PASSPORT FREE ZONE BETWEEN GEORGIA AND RUSSIA – IN RETURN FOR SOUTH OSSETIA REMAINING PART OF GEORGIA

MANTRA

- FRIENDS DO THINGS TO EACH OTHER FOR FREE

RWANDA

QUESTIONS

- HOW CAN INTERNATIONAL ORGANISATIONS DEAL WITH RADIO AND TELEVISION PROGRAMMING THAT ARE INCITING HATRED – CAN YOU GIVE EXAMPLES FROM OTHER COUNTRIES

IDEAS

- RWANDA BURUNDI AND UGANDA COULD JOIN TOGETHER AS ONE COUNTRY TO COMPENSATE FOR AN OVERCROWDED POPULATION. THE AU COULD ASSIST IN THIS.
- INTERVIEWS WITH UN OFFICIALS ON RADIO AND TELEVISION
- IF CHILDREN WEAR SCHOOL UNIFORMS THEY ARE MORE LIKELY TO STAY IN SCHOOL

SAUDI ARABIA

QUESTIONS

- KHADIJA WAS A BUSINESS WOMAN – WHAT KIND OF PRECEDENTS EXIST IN THE KORAN AND HADITH – DEALING WITH THEM. WHAT DID MOHAMMAD SAY ABOUT KHADIJA

IDEAS

- POINT OUT TO THEM – THOSE WHO ARE RICH MUST BE RICH IN GOOD DEEDS
- BREAK THE RULES A FILM ABOUT THE LIFE OF MOHAMMAD – A LOT OF MUSLIMS WOULD APPRECIATE THIS
- THERE SHOULD BE FOUR LAYERS IN THE LEGAL SYSTEM FROM WHICH PEOPLE CAN CHOOSE – TRIBAL ELDERS / IMAMS / JUDICIARY / PRESIDENT
- SAUDI ARABIA SHOULD REWARD ETHIOPIA FOR ALLOWING THE PROPHET MOHAMMED AND HIS FOLLOWERS TAKE REFUGE IN THEIR COUNTRY

MANTRA

- RICH PEOPLE MUST BE RICH IN GOOD DEEDS IF THEY ARE TO MAKE IT TO HEAVEN

SENEGAL

QUESTIONS

- HOW CAN THE EU ASSIST THIRD WORLD NGOS – WHAT EXPERIENCE DOES IT HAVE

IDEAS

- THE UN SHOULD LAUNCH SATELLITES TO HELP AFRICA, THE EU COULD DO THE SAME
- NAVY'S FROM OTHER COUNTRIES ASSISTING AFRICAN COUNTRY'S SUCH AS SOMALIA, SENEGAL.

SERBIA

QUESTIONS

- HOW CAN SERBIA MAKE FRIENDS AND HOW DOES IT DEAL WITH ITS PAST

- HOW CAN SERBIA VET PROSPECTIVE RADIO STATIONS
- WHO CAN HELP SERBIA MAINTAIN THE MEDIAS INTEGRITY

IDEAS

- WHEN ONE PERSON ADMITS TO SOMETHING DONE WRONG IT MAKES IT EASIER FOR OTHER SIDES TO DO LIKEWISE
- THE BRAVEST THING A MUSLIM POLITICAL LEADER CAN DO TO BRING PEACE WITH SERBIA IS TO CONVERT TO THEIR ORTHODOX RELIGION
- POLITICAL LEADERS WHO VISIT SERBIA – SAYING "I HAVE HEARD OF ST. LAZAR – I HAVE READ BOOKS ABOUT HIM"

MANTRA

- ADOPT AT LEAST ONE PASSAGE FROM EVERY RELIGION ON THE PLANET THAT YOU LIKE

SIERRA LEONE

QUESTIONS

- HOW CAN TRIBAL GROUPS IMPROVE THEIR LIVING STANDARDS – HOW CAN GOVERNMENTS ASSIST THEM
- THERE IS NOT ENOUGH MONEY FOR POLICE TO DO THEIR JOB – WHAT KIND OF STANDARDS COULD THEY PRIORITISE

IDEAS

- THOSE RUNNING FOR ELECTION MUST BE LEGALLY REQUIRED TO NOT STATE THEIR RELIGION
- A CITY-STATE INSIDE A CITY JUST LIKE THE VATICAN OWNED BY A FOREIGN COUNTRY – DO THIS FOR YOUR BEST FRIEND. THIS COULD MEAN A BIG BOOST TO THE ECONOMY
- MOST POOR PEOPLE CANNOT AFFORD TO BUY A NEWSPAPER – NGOS COULD PASTE NEWSPAPER ARTICLES ON WALLS
- JOURNALISTS EXPLAINING THEIR ARTICLES TO GROUPS OF PEOPLE – AT SPEAKER OF CORNER SITES IN PUBLIC PARKS

SINGAPORE

QUESTIONS

- "THERE IS A SAYING – YOU CANT TAKE IT WITH YOU" [WHEN YOU DIE]. HOW CAN SINGAPORE USE ITS WEALTH AND EXPERIENCE TO HELP POORER COUNTRIES
- COULD THERE BE A BUSINESS PEACE CORPS FROM SINGAPORE / A UN BUSINESS PEACE CORPS

IDEAS

- POORER COUNTRIES COULD HAVE THEIR OWN UNIVERSITY HOSPITALS
- CHILDREN LIVING AT HOME WITH PARENTS AND GRANDPARENTS ARE LESS LIKELY TO BECOME SINGLE PARENTS
- DO COUNTRIES WANT TO SPECIALISE IN A PARTICULAR TYPE OF MILITARY SUCH AS SOLELY PEACE-KEEPING / DEALING WITH ENVIRONMENTAL ISSUES / RECONSTRUCTION / ACCESS BY THE PUBLIC BARRACKS / REPRESENTING THE PUBLIC IN LEGAL MATTERS

SLOVAK REPUBLIC

QUESTIONS

- WHAT FAMOUS PEOPLE FROM THE SLOVAK REPUBLIC COULD THEIR POLICE FORCE ADOPT AND WORK WITH BOTH AT HOME AND ABROAD

IDEAS

- INHERITANTLY MILITARISTIC NATIONS GET DESTROYED
- THE FUTURE OF THE WORLD IS FORESTS – MOST WORLDS ARE LIKE THIS
- HAVE YOU HEARD OF HER? TRANSLATE HELEN STEINER RICE IN TO OTHER LANGUAGES

SLOVENIA

QUESTIONS

- WHAT KIND OF CULTURAL PRACTICES COULD SLOVENIA ADOPT FROM OTHER ETHNIC AND RELIGIOUS GROUPS TO PROMOTE PEACE WITH THEM - EVEN IF THEY COME FROM OTHER COUNTRIERS – E.G. KIBBUTZ / RAMADAN / PASSOVER / EASTER
- WHAT WORKS FOR TOURISM IN THE MOST SUCCESSFUL COUNTRIES

IDEAS

- GRANTING EQUAL STATUS FOR THE LARGEST ETHNIC GROUPS IN POLITICS
- DON'T HAVE TOURIST STIES MILES AWAY FROM EACH OTHER
- PUBLISHING IN NEWSPAPERS AND BOOKS – TO CORRECT MISPERCEPTIONS ABOUT THEIR COUNTRY
- ANOTHER WAY TO MARKET YOUR COUNTRY IS TO GET SINGERS TO PRODUCE MUSIC IN ENGLISH

SOMALIA

IDEAS

- NGOS INVOLVED IN PEACE MUST BE CHOSEN TO LEAD ALL NEGOTIATONS BETWEEN RIVAL ETHNIC GROUPS IN THE COUNTRY. THE GOVERNMENT DOES NOT PAY THEM WAGES; LOCAL ETHNIC GROUPS FINANCE THEM.
- NEGOTIATORS MUST COME BEFORE PARLIAMENT TO EXPLAIN THEIR DECISIONS.
- IF THERE ARE GOING TO BE PROTESTS ABOUT ELECTIONS. THIS SHOULD BE DEFERRED UNTIL A WEEK AFTER ELECTIONS
- POLITICAL PARTIES THAT SHOULD TRAVERSE COUNTRIES
- EVERY WESTERN NATION SHOULD HAVE BRANCHES OF POLITICAL PARTIES IN AT LEAST ONE THIRD WORLD COUNTRY

SOMALILAND

QUESTIONS

- HOW CAN THE INTERNATIONAL COMMUNITY DEAL WITH THE ISSUE OF THE BREAKAWAY STATE OF SOMALILAND
- WHAT FACTORS COULD BE USED TO DECIDE THE BOUNDARIES BETWEEN DIFFERENT REGIONS

- IF THIS WORLD IS GOING TO GIVE UP WAR – WHAT ARE THE FOUNDING STEPS TO BE TAKEN
- HOW CAN RELIGION DEAL WITH THE ISSUE OF GETTING COUNTRIES TO GIVE UP ALL WEAPONS

SOUTH AFRICA

QUESTIONS

- CRIME IS A BIG ISSUE IN SOUTH AFRICA – WHAT CAN BE USED AS A DETERRENT TO CRIMINALS

IDEAS

- MILITARY TRAINING FOR POLICE

MANTRA

- SA SHOULD USE THE MANTRA "BASES, PRIORITIES, WORTH A SHOT" WHEN SAVING AFRICAN COUNTRIES

SOUTH SUDAN

IDEAS

- JOURNALISTS LIASING BETWEEN REBELS AND GOVERNMENTS – GIVE THEIR OPINION OF THE SITUATION TO EACH SIDE AND BRAINSTORMING IDEAS WITH BOTH SIDES
- IF A COUNTRY IS TO JOIN AN INTERNATIONAL ORGANISATION SUCH AS THE EU – IT MUST HAVE REFERENCES FROM ITS NEIGHBOURING NATIONS

SPAIN

QUESTIONS

- HOW CAN I MAKE SPAIN RELIGIOUS AGAIN.
- WHAT IS THE MISSION STATEMENT / MANTRA FOR TALKS BETWEEN BOTH SIDES
- WHAT ARE THE STRONG CHARACTERISTICS OF MUSLIMS
- HOW MUCH CONTACT HAS THERE BEEN BETWEEN MUSLIMS AND THE WEST

IDEAS

- SEEK TO DO GOOD DEEDS TO MUSLIMS IN WESTERN COUNTRIES AS A PRIORITY – THEN TELL MUSLIMS HOW THESE PEOPLE ARE BEING TREATED. MUSLIMS FROM WESTERN NATIONS WRITING TO MEDIA IN ISLAM ABOUT HOW THEY ARE BEING TREATED
- LANGUAGE TRAINING FOR REFUGEES

MANTRA

- ADOPT AT LEAST ONE PASSAGE FROM EVERY RELIGION ON THE PLANET THAT YOU LIKE

SRI LANKA

QUESTIONS

- WHAT WOULD A PEER-REVIEW MECHANISM FOR THE EU MEMBER STATES LOOK LIKE

- WHAT CAN RELIGIOUS BODIES DO FOR EDUCATION – ESPECIALLY THOSE FROM ANOTHER RELIGION
- HOW CAN SRI LANKA EMPOWER WOMEN IN POLITICS – WHAT EXAMPLES EXIST FOR THIS IN OTHER COUNTRIES
- COULD SRI LANKA ESTABLISH ITS OWN STYLE OF REFERENDUM FOR THE PEOPLE

IDEAS

- BUDDHISTS / MUSLIMS / CHRISTIANS ETC. SHOULD SPECIALISE IN WRITING FICTIONAL STORIES BASED ON FAMOUS PEOPLE IN THEIR RELIGIOUS TEXTS – PEOPLE FROM OTHER RELIGIONS SHOULD READ THEM
- A "CRITICISING AGENCY" WITHIN EACH INTERNATIONAL INSTITUTION SUCH AS THE EU FOR ITS MEMBER STATES

SUDAN

QUESTIONS

- HOW CAN YOU MOTIVATE POLITICIANS ON ALL SIDES TO CHANGE THEIR WAYS NOW
- WHAT CAN BE DONE TO PERSUADE PEOPLE THAT THERE ARE GOOD PEOPLE FROM ALL RELIGIONS
- HOW DO YOU PROMOTE STABILITY IN POLITICS

IDEAS

- PAY NGOS FROM OTHER COUNTRIES TO SET UP A BRANCH IN YOUR COUNTRY AND WORK THERE
- WHEN IT COMES TO A RELIGION – THE MANTRA IS THE MESSAGE REMAINS THE SAME BUT THE MEANS OF DELIVERING IT CHANGES WITH THE TIMES
- GOVERNMENTS COULD PAY FOR THE EDUCATION OF THEIR SOLDIERS – WOULD MAKE THEM MORE RESPONSIBLE IN THEIR WORK

SWEDEN

QUESTIONS

- WOULD THE IRISH SAMARITANS [A FREE COUNSELLING SERVICE] LIKE TO SET UP HERE – THEY ARE RIGHT IN THEIR OPINION THAT COUNSELLING AGENCIES SHOULD NOT TRY TO CONVERT PEOPLE
- WOMEN SHOULD REACH OUT TO MUSLIMS
- THE FOUR BASES FOR SAVING THE WORLD ARE WOMEN / POLICE / CREDIT UNIONS AND NGOS
- WOULD FEMALE ROYALTY REACH OUT TO MUSLIMS BY WEARING THE HIJAB
- MUSLIMS IN THE WEST COULD REACH OUT AS AMBASSADORS TO ISLAMIC COUNTRIES – CHOSEN BY THE GOVERNMENT
- COPY CANADA'S POLICIES FOR TREATING MINORITIES AND IMMIGRANTS

MANTRA

- THE CHURCH MUST BE VISIBLE ON THE GROUND – WEARING RELIGIOUS CLOTHING IF IT IS TO BECOME RELEVANT TO PEOPLE

SWITZERLAND

IDEAS

- EVEN IF YOU HAVE DONE NOTHING WRONG STILL APOLOGISING BECAUSE YOU ARE UNHAPPY ABOUT HOW THINGS TURNED OUT
- ROYALTY AND PARLIAMENT SHOULD BE IN THE SAME BUILDING
- PHARMCEUTICAL COMPANIES COULD GIVE MEDICINES FOR FREE TO THIRD WORLD COUNTRIES, FROM SUCH COUNTRYS AS UK. FRANCE AND GERMANY WHO WOULD FINANCE THIS

MANTRA

- REGISTERING AND TRACKING OF ARMS DEALERS AND THEIR ACTIVITIES ALL OVER THE WORLD

SYRIA

IDEAS

- EACH MUSLIM GROUP IN THE COUNTRY SHOULD ADOPT SOME RELIGIOUS PRACTICES OF THE OTHER SIDE – E.G. PRAYERS – YOU CAN PROBABLY FIND HADITH ON ALL SIDES CALLING FOR TOLERANCE / PEACE ABOVE WAR / FORGIVENESS | A COMMON EDUCATION FOR THE FIRST FEW YEARS OF SCHOOLING – A COMMON RELIGIOUS EDUCATION
- GOVERNMENT / REBELS BOTH STATING THAT REFUGEES WILL BE ABLE TO RETURN TO THIS COUNTRY AND THAT THEY WILL NOT BE ANGRY AT THEM FOR WHATEVER SIDE THEY CHOSE
- AN INTERIM PARLIAMENT BEFORE ELECTIONS – WHO WOULD APPOINT MEMBERS – THE CHURCHES / THE MILITARY / NGOS / BUSINESS LEADERS / FAMOUS PEOPLE / RETIRED POLITICIANS / MINORITIES / TEACHERS / A YOUTH PARLIAMENT.
- AS A CONFIDENCE BUILDING MEASURE – ALLOW FOREIGN POLITICIANS VISIT POLITICAL PRISONERS IF THIS IS THE START OF PEACE
- A PRESIDENT AND A PRIME MINISTER WITH POWERS TO APPOINT MINISTERS. POWERS SIMILAR TO RUSSIA
- RUSSIAN TROOPS IN SYRIA NOT USED – THEIR PRESENCE CAN BE USED AS A DETERRENT TO END THE WAR
- THE LEADER OF THE SMALLEST GROUP IN PARLIAMENT IS CHOSEN AS PRESIDENT
- WOULD PRESIDENT BASHAR AL ASSAD LIKE TO CREATE A FOUNDATION WHEN HE LEAVES OFFICE – MIKHAIL GORBACHEV DID THE SAME. DOES IRAN WANT TO CONTRIBUTE HERE FINANCIALLY TO SUCH A FUND
- AN INNOCULATION PROGRAM TO START A CEASEFIRE
- A PEACE CITY – NO WEAPONS ALLOWED – ONLY POLICE PRESENT AND THEY ARE UNARMED TOO. THE CITY CHOSEN SHOULD BE THE CITY CLOSEST TO THE BOUNDARY BETWEEN THE TWO SIDES THAT HAS REMAINED THE SAME FOR THE LONGEST PERIOD OVER THE LAST SEVEN YEARS
- INVITE UNESCO TO SET UP A PERMANENT BASE IN SYRIA
- SYRIA COULD JOIN THE EUROPEAN SPACE AGENCY
- BASHAR CAN RUN FOR RE-ELECTION IF ELECTIONS ARE SOON
- CIVIL SERVANTS MAKE GREAT NEGOTIATORS
- MILITARY TO MILITARY TALKS
- THE LEADER OF THE SMALLEST ELECTED PARTY AFTER ELECTIONS IS APPOINTED PRESIDENT

- IMMEDIATELY THE REBELS CAN SET UP THEIR OWN CONSULATES IN OTHER COUNTRIES – THESE OFFICES CANNOT BE USED FOR FUND-RAISING THOUGH
- THIS DOES NOT HAVE BE QUID PRO QUO – SYRIAN GOVERNMENT CAN EXCHANGE MEDICAL AID IN RETURN FOR PRISONERS
- ELECTED PEOPLE ARE PUT BEFORE AN ASSEMBLY OF CIVIL SOCIETY FOR THEM TO CHOOSE FROM
- IMAMS CAN BECOME LEADERS OF TOWNS UNDER A CERTAIN SIZE
- MILITARY LEADERS CAN ENTER POLITICS IF THEY RETIRE FROM THE ARMY
- RELIGIOUS PARTIES CAN BE FORMED COMPRISING OF RELIGIOUS CLERICS ONLY
- THE UK SHOULD TAKE FULL CONTROL OF MEDIATING NEGOTIATIONS IN SYRIA – QUID PRO QUO WHERE EACH SIDE HAS ITS OWN SUPPORTERS IS NOT WORKING
- AGREE IN ADVANCE THAT BOTH SIDES WILL AT SOME STAGE DISARM THEIR WEAPONS BY FIGHTERS HANDING OVER THEIR WEAPONS TO THEIR LEADERS FOR THEM TO DEAL WITH
- BONUS SEATS IN A PARLIAMENT FOR PARTIES THAT ACHIEVE PEACE / CEASE FIGHTING SOONEST
- TEN PERCENT OF REBELS MAY JOIN THE ARMY IF THERE IS PEACE AT THE SAME RANKS THEY HELD IN THEIR MOVEMENT
- TAKE YOUR CHOICE PRESIDENT OR PRESIDENTIAL ADVISORS
- RETIRED POLITICIANS RE-ENTERING POLITICS – COULD HAVE A STABILIZING AFFECT ON POLITICS
- THE ALAWITE LANGUAGE IS PRESERVED IN THE CONSTITUTION – ALL CHILDREN MUST LEARN THIS LANGUAGE ALONG WITH THEIR OWN.
- RELIGIOUS LEADERS MUST RECEIVE AN INCOME FROM THE GOVERNMENT NO MATTER WHAT THRIR RELIGION.
- REBELS MAY NOT ENTER POLITICS THEMSELVES BUT THEY CAN NOMINATE THOSE THEY WANT TO RUN FOR THEM
- SYRIA WOULD BE GIVEN A MEMBERSHIP ON THE UN SECURITY COUNCIL IF THERE IS PEACE
- PRESIDENT ASSAD COULD BE GIVEN A POST AS SYRIAS UN AMBASSADOR
- WOULD THE IDA [IRELAND] LIKE TO CONTACT PRESIDENT ASSAD NOW ABOUT DEVELOPING THEIR ECONOMY AFTER PEACE
- BASHAR CAN INSIST THAT BEFORE HE LEAVES OFFICE A LIST OF THINGS HE WANTS IMPLEMENTED AFTER HIM
- EVERY MEMBER OF PRESIDENT BASHARS FAMILY CAN RUN FOR ELECTION
- DOES SYRIA WANT TO CONTRIBUTE TO UN PEACEKEEPING OPERATIONS
- A LIST OF PEOPLE WHO ARE PROTECTED – JUDICIARY / RELIGIOUS LEADERS / POLITICIANS / CIVIL SERVANTS IF THERE IS A PEACE AGREEMENT FOR BITH SIDES
- WIVES ON BOTH SIDES EXCHANGING GIFTS DURING A PEACE AGREEMENT
- A PAGE EACH IN NATIONAL NEWSPAPERS FOR INTERVIEWS WITH MILITARY AND POLITICAL PERSONNEL FROM BOTH SIDES
- BOTH SIDES AGREEING TO APOLOGISE FOR CIVILIAN CASUALTIES
- RELIGIOUS LEADERS ON BOTH SIDES PARTICIPATING IN NEGOTIATIONS
- A BURNING UNIFORMS CEREMONY IF PEACE IS AGREED
- A PEACE BOOK WRITTEN BY CHILDREN IF THERE IS PEACE

MANTRA

- MAKING AMENDS AND NOT PUNISHMENT – EACH SIDE COULD DO THIS – THE UN COULD HELP DRAW UP A LIST OF IDEAS TO BE IMPLEMENTED

TAIWAN

QUESTIONS

- HOW CAN THE EXAMPLE OF HONG KONG BE USED TO DEAL WITH TAIWAN
- WHAT CAN TAIWAN DO WITHIN THE BOUNDARIES OF CHINA – INVESTMENTS / COMMUNITY / SOCIAL JUSTICE / AGRICULTURE
- WHAT KIND OF CULTURAL PRACITICES COULD CHINA MIMIC THAT EXIST IN TAIWAN
- HOW HAS THE CATHOLIC CHURCH HELPED COUNTRIES LIKE CHINA
- HOW CAN CHINA MIMIC THE POLITICAL SYSTEMS IN TAIWAN – WHAT CHANGES WOULD THEY MAKE
- WHAT CAN BE LEARNED FROM THE ERASMUS PROGRAMME IN TH EU FOR STUDENTS

IDEAS

- A SINGLE MILITARY FOR TAIWAN / CHINA
- TAIWAN CAN APPOINT MEMBERS TO THE CHINA PARLIAMENT
- TAIWAN CAN ALLOW IN STUDENTS ON EXCHANGE FROM CHINA
- TAIWAN COULD SHARE JOINT FOREIGN EMBASSIES WITH CHINA

TAJIKISTAN

QUESTIONS

- WHAT ALTERNATIVE USES COULD BE USED FOR POPPY PLANTS – WHAT RESEARCH CAN BE DONE HERE. – PRAGMATISM HERE – FAMERS ARE NOT GOING TO STOP GROWING WHAT IS A LUCRATIVE PLANT

IDEAS

- APOLOGISING FOR NOT HONOURING A PEACE AGREEMENT – SOMEONE OUTSIDE HAS TO PUT PRESSURE ON ALL SIDES TO IMPLEMENT THE AGREEMENT
- RUSSIA COULD RENT AN AIRPORT IN TAJIKISTAN
- SOMEONE HAS KEEP A RECORD OF POLITICS IN A COUNTRY. SOMEONE SHOULD SEEK TO MAINTAIN CONTACTS WITH ALL POLITICIANS AND NOTABLE PEOPLE WITHIN THIS COUNTRY
- A TRADE FAIR WHERE MOST NOTABLE / SPORTS / FAMOUS / POLITICAL PEOPLE FROM THIS COUNTRY ARE PRESENT – FOR TOURISTS FROM OTHER COUNTRYS

TANZANIA

IDEAS

- ASK THE TOURISM AGENCY IN IRELAND TO ASSIST YOU IN TOURISM
- KEEP THE MILITARY BUSY GET THEM INVOLVED IN UN PEACEKEEPING MISSIONS – WOULD INSTILL A SENSE OF PRIDE AND INTEGRITY IN THEM
- TOURIST AMENITIES SHOULD BE CLOSE TOGETHER IN A CITY
- JOINT PARTNERSHIPS ONLY BETWEEN BUSINESS AND GOVERNMENT TO EXPLOIT RESOURCES – COULD REDUCE CORRUPTION

THAILAND

QUESTIONS

- HOW CAN THE WIFE OF THE PRESIDENT SUPPORT SOCIETY – DO GOOD WORKS

IDEAS

- A CERTAIN PERCENTAGE OF RETIRED GENERALS CAN RECEIVE SEATS IN PARLIAMENT
- FRANCHISING – THIS COUNTRY BUILDING AUTOMOBILES ON A LICENCE FROM MANUFACTURER

TUNISIA

IDEAS

- RESTORATION OF RELIGIOUS / HISTORICAL / CULTURAL SITES – IMAMS EXPORTING THEIR RELGIOUS VALUES TO OTHER MUSLIM COUNTRIES

TURKEY

QUESTIONS

- WHAT CHANGES WOULD THE EU LIKE TO SEE IN TURKEY
- WHAT CAN BE DONE TO HELP KURDS ACCEPT STAYING PART OF TURKEY

IDEAS

- INSTEAD OF RESTRICTING MEDIA – THE MEDIA CAN CRITICISE POLITICIANS BUT POLITICIANS HAVE A RIGHT OF REPLY
- THERE SHOULD BE A RIGHT OF REPLY FOR PEOPLE THAT JOURNALISTS TALK ABOUT
- A SECOND SITE FOR MUSLIMS TO VISIT – MEDINA AS WELL AS MECCA – WHY BECAUSE MOHAMMED VISITED THERE TOO. MUSLIMS COULD ALSO VISIT JERUSALEM. MUSLIM CLERICS ISSUING A FATWA SAYING PEOPLE CAN VISIT MEDINA
- A MANTRA FOR MUSLIMS – THE MESSAGE REMAINS THE SAME BUT THE MEANS OF DOING SO CHANGES WITH THE TIMES" THIS COULD HELP BRING WORLD PEACE
- NO ONE SHOULD TAKE PRIDE IN HAVING NUCLEAR WEAPONS – IT IS NOT A MODERN SOCIETY TO HAVE NUCLEAR WEAPONS. IRAN HAS STATED THAT NUCLEAR WEAPONS ARE AGAINST ISLAM.
- A PASSPORT FREE ZONE BETWEEN IRAQ AND TURKEY – KURDS COULD BENEFIT FROM THIS
- THE MANTRA FOR TURKEYS KURDS SHOULD BE "I CANT MAKE YOU FREE BUT I CAN MAKE YOU FEEL FREE"
- COUNTRIES RECRUITING LOCALS AS AMBASSADORS
- JOINT MILITARY EXERCISES BETWEEN NATO AND OTHER NATIONS
- A CYCLING COMPETITION FOR TURKEY SIMILAR TO THE "TOUR DE FRANCE"
- MOBLITY IS THE NUMBER ONE ISSUE FOR BREAK-AWAY REGIONS

TURKMENISTAN

QUESTIONS

- WHAT ARE THE THINGS THAT MATTER MOST TO MUSLIMS

IDEAS

- ADOPTING THE LATIN ALPHABET – WOULD INTEGRATE THIS COUNTRY INTO THE WEST AND BOOST TRADE
- LANGUAGE SCHOOLS IN YOUR BIGGEST TRADE PARTNER

UGANDA

QUESTIONS

- LEARN TO BE CRITICAL OF NATIONS THAT ARE IN THE CATEGORY OF "ROOM FOR IMPROVEMENT" – A PHRASE THE INTERNATIONAL COMMUNITY SHOULD ADOPT

IDEAS

- INTERNATIONAL COMMUNITY MUST PUT PRESSURE ON THIS COUNTRY TO END ARMS FOR MINERALS TRADING IN NEIGHBOURING DRC
- THE LEADER OF A POLITICAL PARTY AND THE LEADER OF A COUNTRY MUST NOT BE THE SAME
- SELL OUT OF SEASON VEGETABLES TO EUROPE

MANTRA

- SHARE POWER WITH YOUR POLITICAL ENEMY – LOVE EVEN FOR YOUR ENEMY IS WHAT IS GOING TO SAVE THE WORLD

UK

QUESTIONS

- HOW DO YOU PROMOTE WOMEN IN POLITICS
- WHAT NEW POWERS COULD THE QUEEN BE GIVEN
- HOW CAN THE UK EMPOWER OTHER NATIONS
- HOW CAN UNIVERSITIES IN THE UK EMPOWER OTHER NATIONS

IDEAS

- ROYAL FAMILY MEMBERS CAN BE CATHOLIC
- THIS COUNTRY SHOULD ENCOURAGE THE REINSTATEMENT OF ROYALTY TO OTHER COUNTRIES IN THE WORLD – PEOPLE LOVE ROYALTY
- THE UK CAN STILL HAVE OBSERVER STATUS AT EU MEETINGS
- THE QUEEN BEING HEAD OF THE SCOUTING MOVEMENT IN THE UK
- **GREAT** BRITAIN
- DIVIDING TERRITORY – TERRITORY OR RESOURCES
- CONTIGUITY – FOLLOWING NATURAL FEATURES – ROADS / RIVERS / MOUNTAINS
- ALIGNING TERRITORY – WHO HAS BEEN THERE LONGEST OVER THE LAST 100 YEARS
- A PEACE IDEA – FROM MARK TWAIN – "WRITING IS EASY ALL YOU HAVE DO IS REMOVE THE WRONG WORDS"

MANTRA

- PROMOTE THE MESSAGE "FRIENDS OR POWER" OUT THERE TOO

UKRAINE

QUESTIONS

- HOW CAN YOU RESOLVE THE ISSUE OF CIS STATES WANTING TO BE PART OF THE EU AND THE CIS
- WHAT KIND OF IDEAS COULD THE CIS ADOPT FROM THE EU

IDEAS

- AN ERASMUS SCHEME FOR THE CIS
- IN IRELAND ST PATRICKS DAY IS CELEBRATED IN OTHER COUNTRYS AND THE TAOISEACH VISITS THE USA ON THIS DAY. COULD THE ULRAINE DO LIKEWISE WITH RUSSIA FOR A SPECIFIC FESTIVAL
- FORMER PROTESTORS FROM ORANGE REVOLUTION CONTINUING TO DISTRIBUTE NEWSLETTERS
- POLITICIANS LOVE PRESS CONFERENCES - UKRAINE AND RUSSIA TOURING OTHER COUNTRIES AND HOLDING JOINT PRESS CONFERENCES - MEMBERS OF THE EU COULD DO THE SAME
- WORLD LEADERS COULD DECLARE NUCLEAR WEAPONS AS EVIL. OVER TIME THEY COULD DECLARE OTHER WEAPONS SUCH AS LANDMINES AS EVIL TOO
- AN INTERNATIONAL SPACE AGENCY FOR THE CIS

UNITED ARAB EMIRATES

QUESTIONS

- HOW CAN THE UAE GET MORE INVOLVEMENT FROM ITS PEOPLE IN GOVERNANCE
- HOW COULD THE UAE ENCOURAGE PARTICIPATORY BUDGETING
- WHAT KIND OF HELP COULD ROYALTY GIVE TO POOR PEOPLE IN OTHER COUNTRIES
- WHAT DO YOU THINK - ARE WOMEN SUPPRESSED TOO MUCH – WHAT KIND OF CHANGES COULD BE MADE – YOU HAVE TO LIST THE RESTRICTIONS AND CHOOSE TO "BREAK THE RULES" ON THEM.

IDEAS

- I AM NOT OPPOSED TO THE HIJAB – MUSLIM WOMEN FREELY WEAR THIS
- ISLAM SHOULD BE CONCERNED WITH MORE THAN JUST MUSLIM COUNTRIES WHEN IT COMES TO SUPPORTING NGOS / CHARITIES IN THE WORLD
- USING NAMES AND SYMBOLS FROM THE KORAN / HADITH TO NAME STREETS AND BUILD MONUMENTS / STATUES
- THE QUEEN COULD VISIT ARAB COUNTRIES - MUSLIMS KNOW THEIR HISTORY AND HAVE HEARD OF LAWRENCE OF ARABIA
- "BREAK THE RULES - BE THE FIRST TO DO THINGS - WOMEN NOT HAVING TO WEAR THE BURKA JUST THE HIJAB ETC. ALLOWING IN YOUTUBE / GOOGLE / WIKIPEDIA
- FORMER POLITICAL LEADERS COULD PLAY A KEY ROLE IN SAVING THE PLANET
- THIS COUNTRY SHOULD SEEK TO HAVE THE BEST JUDICIAL SYSTEM ON THE PLANET
- WHAT KIND OF FATWAS COULD MUSLIM CLERICS ISSUE TO PROMOTE PEACE IN THE WORLD
- HOW CAN MUSLIM CLERICS BECOME ROLE-MODELS FOR YOUNG PEOPLE

URUGUAY

IDEAS

- ASSISTING IN TRAINING OF MILITARY FOR PEACEKEEPING MISSIONS – IRELAND COULD HELP WITH THIS – SMALL NATIONS ARE GOING TO SAVE THE WORLD BECAUSE THEY ARE NOT INTERESTED IN POWER AND MORE INTERESTED IN FRIENDSHIPS / GOOD WORKS

USA

QUESTIONS

- THE MEDIA IN THE USA IS CONTROLLED BY BIG BUSINESS – WHAT CAN BE DONE TO PREVENT THIS FROM HAPPENING IN OTHER COUNTRYS

IDEAS

- THE PRESIDENT SHOULD DO ONE GOOD DEED EVERY DAY FOR THE WORLD
- TIME TO INVESTIGATE HOW TO CLEAN UP RIVERS - HOW MUCH WOULD STRAW HELP
- MUSLIM LEADERS COULD STATE THAT IT IS AGAINST ISLAM TO HAVE NUCLEAR WEAPONS
- PAKISTAN, RUSSIA AND CHINA COULD BE THE FIRST NATIONS TO GIVE UP NUCLEAR WEAPONS - BIG FRIENDS WILL PROTECT US

UZBEKISTAN

IDEAS

- WANTS TO ESTABLISH A TRADE ROUTE ACROSS CENTRAL ASIA – ASSIST WITH THIS FROM THE MIDDLE EAST / EUROPE TO CHINA

VATICAN

IDEAS

- THE CHURCH SHOULD BOAST ABOUT THE GOOD WORKS IT IS DOING IF IT IS TO BE RELEVANT TO PEOPLE
- THE CHURCH SHOULD WEAR RELIGIOUS CLOTHING IF IT WANTS TO BE VISIBLE AND RELEVANT TO SOCIETY
- PEOPLE HAVE TO REALISE THAT IT IS WHAT YOU PUT INTO MASS AND NOT WHAT YOU GET OUT OF IT THAT MATTERS MOST
- PRODUCING THEATRE / PLAYS BASED ON PARTS OF THE BIBLE / KORAN / TORAH – A THEATRE COMPANY SPONSORED BY THE GOVERNMENT TO PRODUCE PLAYS FROM ALL THREE FAITHS – FOR ISLAM THIS WOULD BE BREAKING THE RULES BUT THEY ALREADY PRODUCE BOOKS ABOUT MOHAMMAD AND KHADIJA
- THE POPE SHOULD INTERCEDE IN SITUATIONS OF POTENTIAL CONFLICT – VISITING AND STAYING IN THE CAPITAL OF THE ENDANGERED COUNTRY – NO ONE IS GOING TO STRIKE A CITY WITH THE POPE IN IT – COULD OTHER RELIGIONS DO LIKRETHEM

MANTRA

- CONTRACEPTION INHIBITS SEXUALITY
- THE MORNING AFTER PILL SHOULD BE AVAILABLE TO YOUNG PEOPLE

VENEZEULA

QUESTIONS

- WHAT WOULD PERSUADE A POLITICAL LEADER TO RETIRE WILLINGLY

IDEAS

- RELIGIOUS GROUPS SHOULD BE ALLOWED TO PROTEST AS A GROUP

YEMEN

QUESTIONS

- WHICH MUSLIM COUNTRY WANTS TO BE FIRST TO CHAMPION WOMANS RIGHTS

IDEAS

- MAYBE SOUTH YEMEN AND NORTH YEMEN SHOULD BE BROKEN UP AGAIN
- THE SECOND LARGEST ETHNIC GROUP GETS THE SAME NUMBER OF SEATS IN PARLIAMENT AS THE LARGEST GROUP
- FORMER POLITICIANS AND FORMER LEADERS BEING RECRUITED TO LOBBY FOR YOUR COUNTRY
- A STUDENT SITE FOR PUBLISHED THESIS ACROSS THE MIDDLE EAST

ZAMBIA

QUESTIONS

- HOW CAN NGOS ASSIST THIRD WORLD COUNTRIES TO BROADEN THEIR LIST OF FREE TRADE PRODUCTS

IDEAS

- INDIVIDUAL NAMES INSTEAD OF NAMES OF ORGANISATIONS AT UN SECURITY COUNCIL MEETINGS AND AT NEGOTIATIONS
- LOCAL CHURCHES LISTING THE NAMES OF LOCAL CIVILIANS KILLED BY TRIBAL GROUPS
- FRIENDS CAN DIFFER AND STILL REMAIN FRIENDS

ZIMBABWE

QUESTIONS

- HOW COULD ZIMBABWE MAKE AMENDS FOR REMOVING FOR WHITE FARMERS FROM THEIR LANDS AND HOW COULD THEY HELP THEIR TENANTS
- HOW CAN THE BBC AND OTHER NEWS AGENCIES FROM THE WEST PROMOTE JUSTICE AND INTEGRITY IN AFRICAN COUNTRIES

IDEAS

- POOR COUNTRIES COULD CHOOSE TO SPECIALISE IN SOMETHING SUCH AS HEALTH CARE / NGOS / EDUCATION
- RELIGIOUS GROUPS SHOULD SUPPORT VOTING IN LARGE POOR AFRICAN COUNTRIES. PROVIDE FACILITIES SUCH AS THE PRIESTS HOUSE / CHURCHES / MONASTERIES
- SOMEONE TALKING TO ETHNIC TRIBES AND WRITING DOWN THEIR STORIES / THEIR TRADITIONS AND PRACTICES
- FAMOUS PEOPLE SHOULD USE THEIR INFLUENCE TO HIGHLIGHT CAUSES - INCLUDING FORMER POLITICAL LEADERS
- IF YOU ARE LYING ABOUT AN ELECTION RESULT YOU SHOULD NOT BE LEADER
- RELIGIOUS LEADERS AND THEIR FRIENDS SHOULD BE PRESENT AT EVERY POLLING BOOTH

- RELIGIOUS GROUPS CAN DECLARE AN ELECTION AS FAIR OR NOT FAIR
- PEOPLE WHO ARE DOING GOOD IN THE WORLD NOW - THEIR ACTIONS BEING TAUGHT IN SCHOOLS
- TRIBAL GROUPS SHARING THEIR BELIEFS WITH EACH OTHER. ESPECIALLY ON PEACE AND LOVE - GIVING EACH OTHER RELIGIOUS ITEMS. WITNESSES AT EACH OTHERS RITUALS AS GUESTS

www.ingramcontent.com/pod-product-compliance
Lightning Source LLC
Chambersburg PA
CBHW061737250726
48657CB00002B/970